JOURNEYS OF A
Parisdreamer

CLARA HENSHAW &
VENUS HENSHAW

ARCHWAY
PUBLISHING

Archway Publishing books may be ordered through booksellers or by contacting:

Archway Publishing
1663 Liberty Drive
Bloomington, IN 47403
www.archwaypublishing.com
1 (888) 242-5904

Because of the dynamic nature of the Internet, any web addresses or links contained in this book may have changed since publication and may no longer be valid. The views expressed in this work are solely those of the author and do not necessarily reflect the views of the publisher, and the publisher hereby disclaims any responsibility for them.

Any people depicted in stock imagery provided by Getty Images are models, and such images are being used for illustrative purposes only. Certain stock imagery © Getty Images.

ISBN: 978-1-4808-6403-0 (sc)
ISBN: 978-1-4808-6404-7 (e)

Library of Congress Control Number: 2018906842

Print information available on the last page.

Archway Publishing rev. date: 06/27/2018

Acknowledgments

This book would never have been conceived and written if it had not been for the encouragement of the Senior Friend Finder Bloggers (especially the Arkansas Six); my cousin, Elizabeth; friends Cheryl, Statia, Patti, and Ed; my two daughters, M'Shay and Amber; and my sweet personal champion of a husband, Coach. The inspiration of Venus's journey, her radical personality change, and the use of her blogs formed the basis of this endeavor. The blogs that appear in this book are unedited to preserve the unique personality of Paris/Venus.

Special acknowledgments are given to:
M'Shay Callicott: For her computer expertise
Song: "I Will Survive" written by Freddie Perren and Dino Fekaris
SFF Bloggers: For the use of their screen names and replies to Paris.

To my sister, Paris Venus and the use of her blogs.

Prologue

Ronnie stood on a small knoll overlooking the gathering. Lyrics of "Up, up and away, in my beautiful balloon" wafted from an old jam box perched on a blue '05 Maxima. She was pleased and still a little amazed at how many people showed up to honor Paris, giving her the sendoff she had so desired.

Groups gathered to sing along. Others reminisced about this beloved blogger whose influence had rippled all around the globe. Snatches of quiet conversation could be heard. "I can't believe she's gone. The time just went so fast."

"Her blogs would make me laugh so unexpectedly. Remember the one about the bushes?"

"Or cry. Remember the one about the pickle?"

"I think it was that warped humor and rare transparency that made her blogs special. Even the ones about her struggle with pancreatic cancer almost made me forget that …"

Everyone nodded.

Paris's core group of friends, "The Arkansas Six," had a different conversation. "Senior Friend Finders will never be the same. Her southern-lady qualities and quirkiness brought us together."

"I'll miss her low, husky, suggestive voice and her laughter."

"That was our Parisdreamer. A little nice … a little naughty. You never knew what she was going to say, but everyone loved her!"

From up on the knoll, Ronnie took a deep, fortifying breath and dialed Ian's number.

"It's time."

On June 2, 2006, opaque white balloons danced their way into the atmosphere from Canada, Ireland, New Zealand, China, France, Austria, and all over the United States as a tribute. Released—free to bob, dart, or meander; free like the spirit of Parisdreamer.

Ronnie shook her head, still not fathoming how her sister, Paris, could gather so much love and support in such a short span of time. Goodness knows Paris didn't have many friends before Senior Friend Finder. Maybe if she read Paris's blogs she'd have a better understanding. Remembering some of the outrageous, funny, and courageous things she had been privy to during these last six months, Ronnie smiled. Okay, maybe she could understand.

But Paris had not always been so lovable. Her journey began in a very dark place.

Chapter 1

It was three in the morning, and Paris just couldn't cry anymore. She had lost her mother, her father, two husbands, a lover/soul mate, and her boy toy. She was in the middle of one major pity party, and she just couldn't seem to stop. Who was left to need her? Okay, her dog, Frenchie. But truth be known, he was more destructive than lovable. Who wanted her? Yes, she had two wonderful boys, Gary and Barry, from her first marriage, but they had families and troubles of their own. She had a younger sister and only sibling, Ronnie, the "perfect" one, but that thought surely didn't help. This was a pity party, and nothing in her life was any good! No one needed her, and Paris needed to be needed.

As Paris thought over her past, she couldn't remember ever being truly happy. No real childhood, no friends, no one but her mother. Even *that* relationship had been fed by an unhealthy need for each other. No wonder she was warped. It seemed like all she'd ever learned was to dream, scheme, and manipulate. She dreamed about her future, schemed to get rich, and manipulated circumstances to get the perfect husband. What she actually got was the short end of the proverbial stick.

A whining voice inside her head said, *Kill yourself. That would show them!* Pushing Frenchie off her stomach, Paris turned over and tried to ignore that whiney, goading voice. *It wouldn't be the first attempt. Remember the time you slashed your wrists? Maybe an overdose of all those pills you take would do the trick,* the irritating voice persisted. As she pounded her fist into the innocent pillow, Paris muttered, "Over $600 a month on meds to keep me from being crazy, and here I am talking to a voice in my head. Maybe I didn't want to live those times, but I really didn't want to kill myself! I just wanted attention," she added defensively.

Giving up going back to sleep, Paris got up and shuffled to the kitchen. She filled her coffeepot with water, inserted a new filter with way too much coffee, and then flipped the switch. Surely the aroma would chase the voices from her head. At sixty-one, Paris's future looked bleak. She was fat, alone, broke, and facing going back to work. She'd been unable to hold down a job since her breakdown after her mother's death nine years ago. Here it was 2005, and she still hadn't gotten over it. After all, Paris's mother was the one who raised her to believe she was a princess, a southern belle, born to be taken care of by a rich husband. She retreated into her familiar daydream.

She glided along the perfectly manicured lawn, dressed in a sensual green silk day dress that caressed her generous body and matched her emerald eyes. A lovely coordinating parasol and dainty slippers completed her ensemble. As she sipped a mint julep, a handsome young man with a rakish air grabbed her hand and kissed it. "Now, Brett, darling, you mustn't toy with my affections. You know I'm looking to marry someone with large … assets." Others made their way toward her, vying for her attention, so she turned, fluttered her lace hankie, and dropped it. Shrugging her shoulders, a practiced move to lift her generous breast, she put forward her best damsel-in-distress look and was gratified by the number of young men rushing to her aid. Meanwhile, her eyes roamed to once again admire her traditional southern mansion with its tall Doric columns gracing the background. Large oaks loomed over the lush green grounds that surrounded the house. Servants scurried everywhere.

Okay, maybe she had added that last part after seeing *Gone with the Wind* one too many times. It fit with the princess bit. Paris also loved daydreaming about traveling to far-off places, jetting first class from one city to the next. On each journey, she always included her beloved namesake city of Paris! She drifted off again.

"Fasten your seatbelts" a modulated and very French male voice stated. "We have been cleared for landing at DeGaulle International in just a few moments. Let me personally welcome you to the City of Lights and Love."

Paris flashed him her come-hither smile. He did. "May I be of service to you, mam'selle?"

Idly she reached down and scratched Frenchie's head, grumbling to him, "Not that old dream again. When will I ever face reality? Maybe taking a few extra pills wouldn't be so bad. Who would miss me anyway? Let's get this pity party back on!"

Realizing that the coffee was ready, Paris rinsed her cup in hot water to warm it. Then she poured the coffee—hot, strong, and black, just the way she loved it. Nighttime had always been Paris's favorite, most productive time. No wonder she couldn't keep a day job. She thought so much better at night. Her mind jumped to Murphy's Law. Paris believed in thinking of the worst-case scenarios in all situations. Take this offing herself thing. It would be just her luck to be found in the nick of time, taken to a hospital, have her stomach pumped, and be presented with an astronomical bill for the emergency room. Of course, if they could remove the excess fat while they were pumping her stomach—or perhaps meet a rich, eligible doctor tenderly leaning over her bed …

More than likely, she wouldn't be discovered for several

months. Then she would forever be remembered as that poor, stinking corpse, complete with maggots crawling out of her nose and her faithful little dog rotting beside her. "I've definitely been watching too many police stories, and what a macabre sense of humor, even for me. Well, maybe not," she conceded.

By this time, Paris was on her third cup of coffee. She was too restless to do herself in and too depressed over her old friend Murphy and his fiascos. She padded down the hall, turning on every light in the house until she came to the small bedroom that had recently been refurbished into an office. Her eldest son, Gary, had dropped by last Wednesday, just long enough to set up her old computer—a gift from her stepdaughter, just two years her junior—and help her move furniture around. The stepdaughter was courtesy of her much older, now dead, second husband. At least she had once been called a trophy wife or the younger woman. That marriage should have been her fairy tale come true. It turned out to be another depressing story best left for later. Hello, Murphy's Law!

Paris pushed the button that turned the monitor on, fired up the CPU, and stared at the screen. She was getting pretty good at this Googling stuff. She wondered if there was anything out there for an old, lonely, depressed, fat lady. "Come on, Frenchie. Hop up and we'll see." Senior Friend Finder popped up on the screen. "A dating site for old people? Let's see. Three levels of membership, and the lowest level doesn't cost. Even we can afford that, Frenchie." Paris clicked on the icon to fill out her profile:

> Sex: When I get a chance. Okay, female.
> Age: 61
> Marital status: Widowed
> Hair: Blonde
> Eyes: Emerald green

Weight: Generously curvy
Preferences in a partner: Definitely male,
nonsmoking, must have own hair and teeth,
rich!

Frenchie whined and squirmed on Paris's lap. "Don't lecture me, Frenchie. A woman has to keep some of her dreams!" Scrolling through the profiles of others, Paris noted several men whose profile looked interesting. Of course, they could all be lying. This anonymity was thrilling but double edged. No one really knew. Paris clicked back to her profile screen, made a few adjustments, and then proceeded to check out the rest of the site. Most people flocked to a place called the Lobby. It reminded Paris of a giant cocktail party where everyone made small talk about a variety of topics while checking each other out. It even had the party wallflowers. Here they were called lurkers, and they just hung around listening but not saying anything. Paris lurked awhile and then moved to the quieter conversation area called the Gazebo. She discovered this was the place to go and have a good conversation with just a few friends. Next was the Boudoir. Paris snickered; it was evidently okay there to have titillating conversations and make plans for cybersex. Bizarre!

"Oh my, Frenchie! What have we stumbled onto? A whole new world, and I don't even have to get out of the house!"

From the chat rooms, Paris clicked on Blogs. As Paris scanned the different pages, she deduced that blogs were a place where people expressed opinions or just wrote stuff about life. Then others would post comments.

"No way," Paris uttered. "My fragile ego would never survive under the criticism of others."

Frenchie made a strange yowl as if to agree. As Paris read through the latest posts and replies, she began to get the feel and style of individual bloggers. She also discovered that the comments were more like encouragements from others, relating similar experiences or giving advice. Almost like friends hashing things out in live conversations. Self-help, group therapy, friends discussing life—all in one anonymous spot.

"Interesting," Paris yawned. She would have to think about this. Paris logged off the site, shut down the computer, slipped on her house shoes, and went to let Frenchie out. While he was doing his business, Paris filled his food bowl with Kibbles and gave him some fresh water. Glancing at the clock, she was surprised to see it was almost seven in the morning. She gave in to another yawn. Opening the french doors that replaced her old sliding ones, she called to Frenchie. Then she padded back down the hall with Frenchie nipping at her heels. Falling into bed, Paris realized it wasn't depression she was feeling now but a glimmer of anticipation.

"I'll think of that tomorrow," she said in her best Scarlett O'Hara style. The voices were still now, so she pulled the covers over her head and drifted off to sleep.

Chapter 2

Paris came awake to the sounds of crashes, growling, and frantic barking. Her heart was pounding. What was going on in the kitchen to cause Frenchie to go so crazy? Someone must have broken in! Sure, the neighborhood was slipping downhill, but beggars couldn't be choosers. What irony if she, who didn't have a job, an extra dime to her name, or the proverbial pot to piss in, was being robbed. Maybe she was going to be tied up or even ravished! Should she dial 911? More awake now, she could hear Frenchie's nails scratching on the hardwood floor. His panting and growling indicated he was dragging a treasure, not an intruder, toward his mistress. Paris lay back and took a steadying breath as the panic of Murphy passed.

"Frenchie!" Paris called sternly, in her gravely, just-awake voice. "You've been up on my table again! You bad boy, dragging my purse down the hall like that and scaring me to death. I guess you want me to get up, don't you, boy? Okay, I'm getting up."

Paris heaved herself out of bed and started her daily routine: Let Frenchie out. Get her coffee. Let Frenchie in. Move to the bathroom for her morning constitutional. Shower. Then, because she was going out of the house, she even put on makeup.

Next, more coffee. She pulled off her caftan, dragged on her sweats, and fixed her hair. Finally, an hour and a half later, she picked up her car keys and her purse, said good-bye to Frenchie, and started out on her much-hated weekly trip. Like it or not, money or not, there were always a few necessities she had to pick up at her local Dollar General. It wasn't far for her to drive, just a few blocks. She maneuvered the car as close to the front door as she could and then parked. She commandeered a cart from the lot, plopped her heavy black purse in the child's seat, and then pushed the cart through the entry. Once inside, Paris meandered her way throughout the store while drifting away in her make-believe world.

An older gentleman with wavy white hair and a gorgeous smile filled with his own gleaming white teeth pulled out his platinum American Express card. "Darling, you must take it! Buy whatever you need. Do not even consider the cost. We will be leaving on our trip to Paris in a few days. You will need lots and lots of new things. Buy yourself some new luggage. Charge anything your heart desires. You deserve to be pampered, my sweet."

Up and down the aisles, Paris dreamed, while selecting her items. It was only when she pushed the cart up to the cashier that she broke out in a cold sweat. She could feel herself shaking all over. Even with so few items, she worried she would not have enough money. It wasn't like she'd splurged on anything, except maybe the jar of Nivea face cream and the package of Werther's Original hard candy. Really, the face cream was an investment in marketing; a necessity, really. After all, she had to look good if she were to find Mr. Right.

The cashier broke into Paris's daydream, "That will be twenty-one dollars and eighty-seven cents."

Paris put forth her crumpled twenty and began digging in her purse. "Eight, nine, ten cents." Shrugging her shoulders,

Paris looked up with tears in her eyes and a quivering smile on her lips. "I'll put something back."

The cashier dug into her uniform pocket and made up the $1.77 difference. Paris glanced at the nametag and said, "Thank you, Veronica. I'll give it back to you when my disability check comes in."

"No need," said Veronica. "I've known hard times myself."

"Thank you," Paris mumbled while picking up her one measly sack.

Safely back at her house, Paris balanced her precious sack of necessities on her ample hip as she simultaneously unlocked the door and stuck one foot out to hold back Frenchie. Jumping up and down and barking his, "glad you're home, got to go out now" bark, the dog made it nearly impossible for her to get into the house. Paris was always very careful not to let him out the carport door, for fear of losing her angel dog.

Frenchie had come to her almost a year ago, a month after breaking up with her young boyfriend she'd dubbed her boy toy. She reflected:

> **I was out in the backyard watering and I felt an overwhelming sense of loss. It almost hurt to breathe! I was up near the spot where I had buried Rollo, the 15 year old Boston terrier that had been my little dead hubby's and my companion. It had almost been a year since I had to have him put to sleep. (My dog, not my hubby!) It was also coming upon the 10 year anniversary of my mother's death. The fact that it was also a Holiday Weekend just seemed to add to my misery. The old black lab next door came close to the fence to be petted. As I was talking to**

her and stroking her head, I started to cry. The tears would not stop. I headed into the house, got some iced tea. I decided to check my email before I went out in the front yard to move the water sprinklers I had no mail! When I finished my tea, I headed out the carport door and for a moment paused, looking across the street at the house where my sister had lived before they built their new home. While I was standing there, something touched the back of my leg and I screamed! There had been some mice in the laundry room. I am just plain "goosey" any way. When I screamed, there was a little "YIP, YIP." I looked down to see a fuzzy little black puppy go up under my car. I finally coaxed him out. I took him around to some of my neighbors to see if he belonged to any of their holiday guests. No one had ever seen him. I called the humane society and the animal control. They were closed. I called the non-emergency police number but no one had reported him missing. I placed an ad in lost and found section of the local paper. No one ever claimed him. It was almost as if my Mother or an Angel had seen my loneliness and had placed him on my carport just for me to have and to love. After about a week I thought up the name Lil' Frenchie.

Yep, that was another one of those days when the voices were gathering and the pity party was gettin' on! Paris shook her head from the memory and scooped up the little dog. She gave him a quick hug before putting him out. It didn't take long to put up the meager groceries. After letting Frenchie back in, Paris snagged her bag of Werther's and headed for her computer. She had thought about Senior Friend Finders all afternoon. Her decision to do the most daring thing she'd ever done was made. These people didn't know her; she didn't know them; she'd never see them. By creating and using a screen name, she felt that she could be free and safe. So, she decided to be her real self on line. Once on the site, Paris navigated to the "write blog" page, selected the size, font, color of type and background, and then began to type:

Smothered By My Mother.

I was my mother's everything, her whole world. I was her real little doll who looked like Shirley Temple! I was born during WW2 and my father was overseas I was raised like an only child- never allowed to play with my sister or others.... just my mother.

I remember when I was about five, my mother and daddy would get in loud arguments and it scared me to death. I still to this day do not like arguments or discord of any kind. When it was really bad, my dad would get his little suitcase, pack it, and start out walking very slowly to our closest bus stop. Mother would calm down and start to cry. Then she would say "Paris, Paris, run get your daddy and tell him to

come back home. Tell him that you don't
want him to go and that you love him. Don't
let him leave us!

So, being the good little girl that I was, I
did that. I was crying by the time I caught
up to him and said "DADDY< DADDY,
Pleeeeeease don't go, don't leave us...please
come home!" By this time I WAS PULLING
AT HIS TROUSER LEG AND CRYING
MY HEART OUT! Looking back, I would
NEVER do this to a child. It was so cruel!
I felt like the whole fate of the family was
all on me. I have tears now as I write this.
But, in a way, I feel better for telling it (like
therapy!).

The next evening, Paris had mixed feelings about checking
on her blog. What if everyone made fun of her or her writing?
What if no one read it? What if— "I might as well check,
Frenchie. It's not as if they know who I am. Let's be brave and
see if anyone has read or responded to my first blog."

She checked the page. "Two hundred twenty-seven
views! Wow!"

Looking at her responses, Paris discovered a feeling of wellbeing. It had been rather cathartic. How supportive everyone
was! They seemed to like her and her writing. She studied the
number of people who had read her blog, reread the comments,
and then checked all of the other new posts to see how theirs
fared. A competitive streak kicked in. She hadn't realized she
even had one. Encouraged and challenged, Paris proceeded to
write about another great hurt that had been festering all her
life, one that had damaged her so badly that it had shaped her

lonely existence. It dealt with her first attempt to break out of her loving but smothering mother's arms and find a friend. Paris knew she needed another good title to draw them in. Color: green; paste a little clip art of a green pickle; add the title:

Paris' Pitiful Tale of the Pickle!

When I entered grade school I had no social skills at all. I did not know how to just be a kid and play. I did not know how to join in and waited out by a tree with my back against it trying to look nonchalant. I thought the kids ought to come and invite me to play! They just ignored me, which after a while made me think that there must be something wrong with me. Everyone else was playing in little groups! I became so sad. My Mother made me feel like the most important person in the whole world! So I became more convinced that something was wrong with me. I wanted so to belong, and did not have a clue. So I began observing the kids. There was this one pretty little girl that everyone seemed to like. She was the one that I wanted to be my friend. She had blonde hair and blue eyes. I noticed that she brought pickles in her lunch. So, with my childish mind, I thought well, she likes pickles: I will bring her a pickle tomorrow and she will like me! The next day, I watched until she was at the drinking fountain by herself. I summoned all the courage up and

tapped her on the back. She turned around and looked at me with those big blue eyes. I said, "Judy, would you be my friend? I brought you a pickle." and I handed her the pickle wrapped in waxed paper. Her eyes got bigger and she had that "deer trapped in a headlight" look, and she ran! She ran to a group of her friends and whispered, and pointed to me, still standing with the stupid pickle in my outstretched hand! That was my first attempt to make a friend.

Hesitantly, Paris clicked on *post*. A tear hit the keyboard. Damn! It still had the power to make her cry. *I wonder if I should go back and delete it. Everyone will think it's so stupid. Only some pitiful idiot would bare their soul to complete strangers.*

She leaned over and scooped Frenchie up. "It's a good thing we have screen names and I don't have to face these people." Cuddling Frenchie and whispering sweet words to him, she finally pushed herself up from the chair. Paris continued to beat herself up as she started her bedtime rituals. It was only 2:00 a.m., but this blog had really drained her.

━━ Chapter 3 ━━

Paris woke to a wet tongue licking her face—Frenchie's, not her handsome dream lover's. "Just my luck." She glanced at the clock. Four in the afternoon and time to get up. She flexed her fingers and then her toes. Next, she rolled over to her back and grunted a few times before heaving herself out of bed. Shuffling to the bathroom, she washed her face and peered into the mirror. *Oh, my God! What was I thinking? How could I tell the world what a pathetic failure I am without having a single friend?*

Hearing Frenchie bark, Paris straightened her shoulders, shook her head, and quoted to herself a line of her niece Nicole's country song, "What is done is done, is done, is done. I'm riding out this flood!"

"I don't care what they think anyway!" Paris stated defiantly aloud. "They aren't real."

Moving to the kitchen, she followed her methodical routine: put the coffee on, let Frenchie out, and warm her cup. After pouring a cup of the hot, black liquid, she let Frenchie back in. She scrounged a bowl of oatmeal and toasted the bread until it was black. Next, she scraped the burn off the toast with a knife and then slathered it with a stick of butter still in the wrapper, just like her mother had always done. It didn't matter that her mother had done it that way because of a toaster that didn't work. It was ingrained in Paris, so she still prepared it the same way.

Once finished with breakfast, she stacked her bowl on top of the other dishes in the sink, poured a final cup of coffee, and made her way to curl up on her sofa in the ten-by-twelve "media room." Formerly, it was a bedroom. The closet had been removed, bookshelves added on either side of the media stand, and the window converted to french doors. She had moved into this house shortly after hubby number two had died. Paris had blown through her half of an inheritance from her father by that time, spent an additional twenty thousand dollars that she didn't have, and then convinced Ronnie to fund the house makeover so she would have a place to live. After enlarging the kitchen, changing the cabinetry from pine to white, adding larger windows over the sink, adding extra lighting and a couple of french doors in the connecting dining area, it was the perfect 1,180-square-foot dollhouse. Rather, it *would* be perfect if she could ever get all of her boxes unloaded. Anyway, with the white and the light, it did offset some of her seasonal depression. How she loved this house! Reluctantly, she admitted that it was good of her sister and brother-in-law to make all the changes and let her live here for free.

Settling back into the couch, Paris turned on the TV and then pursued her favorite alone pastime. She hooked the 10X mirror around her neck, took up her favorite pair of tweezers, and began to pluck everything. Her thoughts drifted to how she'd gone from having a substantial inheritance to being flat broke. Despite her promise to her sister that she could handle the money and deserved to be treated as an adult, it was all gone. Yes, the explanation was simple, really: Burt, boys, and buying. What was that old saying? Easy come, easy go.

"Dad had been right not to leave it to me," Paris mused.

Instead, he'd left Ronnie in charge. Ronnie, his darling. Ronnie, his "can't do anything wrong" little tomboy. Ronnie was short, maybe five feet, with mousey brown hair and prune-brown eyes, the same color as the doorknob in their old Dennison house. *Ronnie always thought I meant her eyes looked like shit, just because the knob just happened to be to the bathroom.*

"Now, I couldn't help that, could I, Frenchie?" Paris asked with a snicker.

"Being a teacher had made Ronnie a bossy little thing, but I digress. Can you imagine, Frenchie, how humiliating it was to ask a younger sister for every dime? What would happen if she died? I still can't believe she gave it to me. I never would have, had our places been reversed. Of course, despite all of her bluster and preaching, she has such a soft little heart that can be so manipulated." Paris smiled as she scratched Frenchie behind his ears. "In hindsight, Ronnie should have stuck to her guns and listened to Dad. But oh, for a time it was so much fun. It made me feel like Ms. Astor! Independent, rich, worthy!"

Paris drifted back, remembering a time before the money, yet at the beginning of the downfall. His name was Burt. She had been looking for a husband and let it be known she was looking for an older man—one with his own hair and teeth … and *rich*. If not rich, able to provide her with a home and amenities. Along came Burt—debonair, charming, witty, and with his own hair and teeth. Not bad looking for a man thirty years her senior either! Up front, she told him what she was looking for and that she had lots of debt. Lots! He took her to the most expensive restaurants, out dancing, and showed her his quaint hilltop home secluded in a great neighborhood.

"I have some really messed-up feelings when I think of Burt," Paris muttered out loud. Putting down her tweezers and picking up Frenchie, Paris continued, "Remember my constant old friend, Murphy, Frenchie? Well, Burt was so good to me and for me. I know he loved me. He respected my mind and wanted the best for me. Yet, I never could get over the fact that he lied to me."

Paris shoved Frenchie from her lap, picked up her tweezers, and started plucking with a vengeance. "Yes, lied! The house belonged to his daughter. Burt had spent all his savings and investments on his first wife's illness. He didn't have anything! Yet, he and his daughter had me sign a prenup. A prenup! Who does that unless they have money? That's why, instead of the trophy wife he married, I fixed him. He ended up with a fat, old slob. Oh, how it infuriated my stepdaughter, the one who was just a few years younger than me. She would come over and see what her poor daddy had to put up with. Dishes in the sink, pans all over the counters, stuff stacked up everywhere, and a very fat wife. Well, tough! At least she would never complain that I wasn't feeding her father or taking care of his every need. As the years passed, I couldn't help but baby him, feed him, care for him. It has always been my nature to care for others. I didn't have to like it. To add insult to injury, he couldn't work anymore."

Frenchie whined and pawed her lap.

"Okay, so he was in his late eighties by then, but he was supposed to take care of me! I had to spend a great deal of my recently acquired inheritance to just pay his medical bills. Then he just died. As much as I resented him, Frenchie, I still loved him, and I was lost.

"I'll never forget that while I was still stunned with the reality of being alone again, I was told by my 'daughter' that I had to move out! Not in six months or three months, but in two weeks! Okay, so maybe my boy toy, Al, might have had something to do with it. But hey, a girl has to do what a girl has to do, right? I thought she understood when I told her about how strong and durable his equipment was. Guess not. As hard as it was for me, I called my sister to ask if I could move here to our parents' home, since it was empty. I was surprised and shocked when she agreed. I guess she really isn't such a bad egg. It was a good decision on my part. I love this place, especially after all the renovations."

Paris shifted positions, changed the channel on the forgotten TV, and plucked some more. Then she drifted back to her thoughts. "After Burt came the buying. The internet made it so easy! I didn't even have to leave the house. My favorite site was Goodwill.com. Instead of the 'debil,' it was my mama's influence that made me do it. She loved the Goodwill. When we were kids, and if it rained, we would load up in our standard-shift, puke-green Pontiac and head for the nearest Goodwill to scour for the latest treasures. All I had to do was click on the computer and search for a thrown away antique treasure to call my own. It gave me such a sense of power! Click, buy, and it was delivered to my door. Now I have boxes and boxes of stuff. Occasionally, when I did feel like getting out, I would get dressed up and go to Dillard's and pretend I was Ms. Astor. It was so much fun. As long as the money lasted, I could buy. I was someone."

Frenchie scratched at the couch and ran to the door and back, trying to get her attention.

"Okay, Angel, I'll get up!" Paris made her way to let Frenchie out and then in. Same routine. How did she get so destitute? *Oh, yeah, Burt, buying, and my boys. Well, no surprises there.*

"What mother wouldn't use a windfall to help her children?" Paris mused. "Ah, well, it was fun while it lasted. I hate to admit I'm broke again, but I wouldn't want to disappoint dear old Dad! With no money for gas, it's a good thing I still have the internet."

Restless and tired of reliving the past, Paris made her way to the kitchen. She nuked a big bowl of Campbell's chicken noodle soup, poured a glass of southern sweet tea, and made her way to the computer.

"I'll just see how my last post did. It's kinda fun posting when no one knows me!"

Wiggling her finger for Frenchie to follow, Paris sat down and sipped on her soup as she navigated to her blog. Choking, Paris called out, "Wha— 783 views!"

Chapter 4

A few months later, Paris was in near-panic mode. A real live blogger from Ireland was coming to Little Rock and had requested for Paris to be his guide. It was hard to wrap her head around a real person being connected to a fictitious blogger name.

"I would have never bared my soul to real people," Paris grumbled. "I've never been good in social situations. I'm horrible with strangers. What can I do?" Paris was really working herself up. "I know! I can always plead sick. Maybe the plague? Okay, the flu! Or I could discover I'm terminal and need to be alone? Hmm, better yet, I have left town to help a dear old aunt. Surely no one really expects me to actually meet this person?"

When Paris received the call to pick up Loth from the airport, she was truly sick from worry. Yet, when she heard his thick brogue, full of the Irish blarney, Paris couldn't resist. Not as another "potential," because everyone in blogland knew that despite the blarney, Loth was happily married to a wonderful, sweet woman. He just seemed fun, comfortable, and like he truly desired to get to know the real bloggers. What if he was disappointed? What if he told everyone how she really looked?

What if—? "No!" Paris scolded herself. "I took a chance online with the real me, and I'm not quitting now."

After Paris's and Loth's road trip to Russellville to meet another blogger and the long wait before the plane left, Paris's nerves were shot. She was totally exhausted. She opened the kitchen door, greeted Frenchie, and took care of his needs. Paris then flopped, fully dressed, onto the bed, pulled the covers up over her head, and closed her eyes. The last thought she had was *Could Loth be right about my whining?*

When Paris woke up, she was not surprised that she'd slept fourteen hours. She did feel surprised, however, at her optimism. "I must be changing, because I didn't wake up defensive, mean, or having 'How dare he?' thoughts," she mused. She couldn't wait to get to her computer and share her experience in her next blog.

> **Almost everyone on SFF knows and loves our Sir Loth from Ireland. You have probably either met him in the chat rooms on SFF, or he is probably best known for the creative, sometimes outrageous blog that he writes for us here in Blog Land! Enjoy him while you can for I predict that not too long from now we will have to buy his book! He is far too talented not to share his tales with the whole WORLD!**
>
> **I was fortunate enough to meet him and be his Little Rock host and Chauffeur. He is happily married to Lady Claude, who must have the patience of a Saint. I feel it must be**

a trait shared by all women who love great and brilliant men! He wanted to come to America to meet some of the friends he has made on SFF. He first flew to NYC to meet his good friend, Andy, his very favorite! He spent several days there. He then flew in to Little Rock, about 11am on Tuesday, and I picked him up at the airport. We drove to Russellville about 77 miles away to meet another friend of ours, Sissy. We toured her Senior Center then went to her home where she demonstrated her ability to ride her little motor scooter! We then went to Ryan's for Lunch! It is a moderately priced buffet style restaurant with a wonderful selection! Another SFF friend, Nancy, was to fly in from Texas Wednesday morning at 11:15. I was the only one with a car. I suggested to Loth that he stay at a motel by the airport with a shuttle service to the airport because he wanted to go meet her flight an hour or two early, in case the plane arrived sooner. He reluctantly agreed, but he said he would give me a hundred dollars to let him sleep on my couch! I said I just could not do that! So, he checked into the Days Inn...I met them both at the airport at 11:30 on Wednesday morning. We then went to the Southwest Little Rock's Ryan since Loth had been so impressed with it the day before in Russellville! We had a lovely, leisurely visit and then got back to the airport about 2:30 for Nancy's 3:30 flight. I told Nancy good-bye and that I would be back at 3:30 to pick up Loth. I made a flying trip home to check on Lil' Frenchie and let him out. Loth's flight left at 7:30 am Thursday morning. It was then about 3:45! As I have mentioned before, my little house is just full of boxes that I have not made much progress with getting unpacked despite my best intentions! There are little trails through the mazes. I was embarrassed and did not want to bring Loth to my house! However, after a frank discussion on the side of the road, tears, and assurances I relented. After all, what were we going to do for nearly 10 hours? I took him to the grocery store and picked up a few items. Then I took him to my house to meet Lil' Frenchie... We had a cheese and onion sandwich that he made with the bread untoasted and lightly buttered! And a beer! Then he insisted in moving some of the boxes that were too heavy for me and took them up to the storage building! He worked until dark with Lil' Frenchie barking at him the whole time and almost nipping his heels until he made friends with him! Then we talked, and talked and talked and talked, etc.! During our frank discussions on many subjects, Loth felt it his duty, as my friend to tell me that if I did not quit my "Whining" and feeling sorry for myself attitude, I might as well be dead! And besides that, I would never get a man! I would be the type person that other people will run from! I am

taking his words very seriously! He also said that I would never get things in my house straightened out if I don't have a strong man to help me move things and to push me. Soon it was about 1:30 AM... he said he would like to go to the airport and maybe get a nap but he did not want to go sleep in a motel, it wouldn't be worth the price. He did not want a nap at my house because he did not want to chance missing his plane. (By then, I was comfortable enough with the kind of person that he was, I would have let him nap.) So, Lil' Frenchie went to the airport with us and we said our goodbyes! We put our good friend out at the door, to fly back to NYC later that morning! From the Airport, Senior Center, Restaurant, Motel, Grocery Store, and Liquor Store for beer, Loth charmed his way into the hearts of the people of Little Rock and I hope the other way around!

After the posting, Paris read through the other blogs and then went to the chat room. Comfortable now, she welcomed newcomers and served as hostess and moderator, moving the conversations on and making sure everyone was included and playing nicely. Several of the regulars decided they should meet in L. R. for a luncheon and get to know one another. Somehow, Paris got volunteered to help with it, even though she'd been taught by her dear old dad never to volunteer. Ah, but then she had always envisioned herself as a sophisticated hostess.

Back at the mansion she glided around the ballroom, meeting each guest by name. "John, how good of you to come. Alice, don't you look divine in your Dior."

In turn, her guests would gush and compliment her. "The floral arrangements are so lovely and lavish! Heavenly!" they exclaimed as each culinary offering was presented by gloved waiters in smart military-style uniforms. "I must have the name of your caterer."

"Is the chef Parisian?"

"How delicious the champagne is! It must be imported."

"You've outdone yourself once again."

Paris smiled and moved on. She joined another adoring group, but all the while, her eyes constantly scanned the gathering for a possible love of her life—or interlude.

Paris's eyes snapped open at the sound of insistent barking. "Okay, Frenchie, so it's a meal at the Golden Corral, on mismatched plates and plastic glasses, not Wedgwood and Waterford at the mansion! At least it's a step in the right direction. I'm getting out! Besides, who knows, my Mr. Rich—I mean Mr. Right—might be there."

Chapter 5

The weeks had flown by. The day of the Little Rock luncheon arrived, and Paris almost missed it. A terrible bout of nerves and indecision about what to wear caused Paris to be physically sick. When she finally pulled herself together and got out the door, Murphy's Law romped, and she lost her way to the restaurant. Despite all the mishaps, Paris pulled into the parking lot ten minutes early. That was certainly a first for her; she was known for being late. A fleeting smile crossed her lips as she thought of how many times her wonderful baked beans arrived at the family gatherings after everyone had finished eating. Yanking her thoughts back to the present, she checked the mirror to see if she needed to apply more lipstick. Arriving early wouldn't help if she kept procrastinating and didn't get out of the car. Folding her arms across the steering wheel, she laid her head down and took a couple of deep breaths. Somewhat recovered, she heaved herself out, checked to make sure she had her keys, and locked the doors. Plastering a welcoming smile on her face, she turned and made her way inside the Golden Corral.

The next afternoon, she returned home after having left
the luncheon with several of the bloggers for a spontaneous
adventure to Hot Springs. Paris couldn't imagine who this
woman was entering her house. Had she really cohosted the
Little Rock luncheon? Driven to Hot Springs in the midst of a
storm? Partied and spent the night away from home? She smiled.
Not too bad for an old, reclusive broad. Yep, she was changing,
and she liked this new woman. She kicked off her shoes, fell
on top of her bed, and pulled an afghan over her. Seven and
a half hours later, she awoke from her nap. Excited about the
events and looking forward to sharing in her blog, Paris didn't
linger in bed as usual but made her way to the kitchen. Feeling
somewhat hungry, she opened the refrigerator and stared at
the near-empty shelves. She turned to the cabinet and removed
a can of tomato soup. While the soup was heating almost to a
boil, she rummaged up the last of the crackers and poured some
sweet tea. After letting Frenchie out for a while, she took her
late supper to the computer. Paris sipped her soup and waited
for the internet to come up. Glancing at the clock, she noticed it
was 11:30 p.m., plenty of time to write and post her latest blog.

> **Well, my friends, you missed a good one! I
> can't upload pictures from this computer, but
> when I go to my sister's house I'll try again!
> Even the ones In Hot Springs! Lol. I arrived
> at the luncheon later than I had planned, but
> about 10 minutes until 12 pm when it was
> scheduled to start. When I arrived, there
> were 3 guest waiting and Fooled Once, the
> host. Of course, as I told you, I was the co-
> hostess for this first Arkansas shindig! Lol.**

The guests that were there had arrived the night before and had spent the night in Hot Springs, AR. They were NancyL who flew in from TX, and LaBella Donna, who picked her up at the airport and had driven in earlier from TX, also. Yellow Duck drove in from Mississippi. They had had a fine ole time in Hot Springs the night before. I don't know everything but I heard there was some expert pool played by Nancy!! We were joined shortly by Arkansas Whistler, A romantic man, Shanda, and then TA DA! Our OWN SCOOTER! I was so pleased! Later, after we had eaten, she entertained us with a few songs on her Harmonica! Then Llinginger came late because he had driven from quite far away and had trouble finding the place! With me, that made 10. I did not count Shanda's daughter and her friend who came with her. They ate in the other part of the restaurant. We all hugged like long lost friends when we met! We were all cordial and had a lovely time chatting and finding out more about each other! It was just like we had known each other forever!

I thought I would be really nervous, but I wasn't. I think we all hated to leave!

Fooled Once, NancyL, La Bella Donna and Ducky all returned to Hot Springs. I went home, gathered up my stuff and Lil' Frenchie and headed South. I stopped by my sister's house to get her cell phone so I could keep in touch with the others. Then I went a little bit further and met my daughter in law and let them keep Frenchie for a few days. Then off I headed to Hot Springs, right into the path of a terrible storm! The road seemed to disappear several times before my very eyes! I had to pull off the road once. A truck almost ran me off the road and there was terrible streaky lightning almost hitting the ground in front of me.

I was trembling mess when I arrived in the Lobby of the Arlington Hotel in Hot Springs. I parked my car in a lot across the street and left it there most all the night. I had a glass of merlot to settle my nerves. Then we made plans. We decided to go to one of Bill Clinton's favorite eating places in Hot Springs, McClard's BBQ! We all laughed and giggled and talked about the rest of you in Blog Land and Chat Land! Lol. We talked about the goodies and the baddies! Lol. Well, some men in the adjoining booth became so interested in the odd names we were mentioning; I smiled and explained we were all Senior Friend Finders friends from the Internet! Lol. You should have seen their, "OH, OKAAAY" looks! From there we went to a club that one of the group was a member. It was Boot Scooters. Normally, I would have been very nervous, and dreaded going into a strange place, but I was not a bit nervous, and was having a wonderful time. Nancy, Belle and I had been in the back seat being naughty and giggling up a storm. The two men, Fooled and Ducky were in front. Fooled was the designated driver and was drinking Cokes (diet, I think). We all went in. Ducky paid the cover charge for all of us. He also bought a round of drinks for us. There was about a 65 year old couple who were the Deejays! They played a great mix of Country and Golden Oldies. It was an older crowd. They really had some wonderful dancers. I got to dance twice. I think Belle did also! Ducky and NancyL did not join in the dancing. Later a live band came on and we stayed for a set. They were pretty good. Then we went to another bar. My niece and her husband are the band, "Texarkana". They were playing at another bar, which did not have a dance floor. It is called, "The Big Chill". There was a large, younger crowd there when we arrived. I was thrilled when we came in because she had just started the song, *Black Velvet*, about ELVIS. When she finished it, she left the stage and came to hug me! I whispered to her to please play *House of the Rising Sun*. She dedicated to me! If you know the song, you will know why that was a bit embarrassing! Lol There was a lady at the bar, who saw all that and came up to me and smiled. She said she was Deborahsu. She could not make it to the luncheon but had "heard" us talking about coming to hear my niece play at this place and had been there an hour or so waiting for us. She drove in from Texas, also! We all ended up sitting out on the covered porch and visiting, laughing, getting to know each other better and having a few drinkie poos! Lol We all hugged and planned to meet at the waffle place across from the Arlington for breakfast at 11AM. We hugged goodbye and they left. I stayed until my niece and her husband left and they took me back to my car. Her hubby rode with me and we followed my niece out to my sister's little cabin on a nearby lake. We stayed up talking about my lovely evening out with my new friends and what a wonderful show they had done! Well, I overslept the cell phone alarm and did not get to meet the others for breakfast. After my niece and her husband left I stayed and made coffee and sat on the screen porch for a few hours and reflected on our first Arkansas Friend Finder Luncheon! The only thing wrong with the whole thing was that you all weren't with us! Lol

Paris posted the description and stretched her arms over her head. Then she leaned back and closed her eyes. *It is so wild to think I actually might have some friends and that they like me. I mean ... me! The fat, finagling, and far outrageous me! We're already planning another get-together in Dallas!*

Paris moved into the kitchen area and sat down on her blue brocade Queen Anne chair. She picked up li'l Frenchie and absently stroked his back. "I have no money for gas, hotel room, or extra food, but I'd really like to go. These people seem to be good for me. I'm nervous about driving that far by myself, and I've never spent the night with strangers. Okay, some I know from the luncheon, but, back to the problem of money. What do you think, Frenchie?"

Woof.

"My sister?"

Woof.

"Now, how can I talk her into footing the bill?"

Woof, grrr.

"Yes, making her feel guilty usually works. I'll remind her how she's always gone off with her friends and done things, but I never got to, especially in high school. I'll remind her about the trip to Natchez that I missed because Mother turned off my alarm. Oh, poor me! Yes, Ronnie always felt bad over that one. It just might work!"

Paris waited until 8:00 a.m. and then picked up her phone and dialed Ronnie's number. Paris laid out her plan, and Ronnie immediately went into her "how irresponsible can you be?" mode. Paris suppressed a sigh. Tuning back in as the conversation slowed, she heard, "The only way I'll consent is for me to take you myself. There is no telling what these people are like! You don't know what you're getting into. There is something in the news every day about bad things happening to people who develop relationships over the internet and leave to parts unknown, never to return!"

When Paris replaced the phone to its cradle, she picked up Frenchie and said, "It's not what I expected, but I get to go! And you, my angel, will need to stay the weekend again with my favorite and only grandson, Chuck. Now, outside with you to do your business, and then I'm off to bed. I must get my beauty sleep and a little energy if I'm to be a gallivanting hostess with the mostest!"

Chapter 6

Several weeks later, after the exhausting and hurried trip to Dallas, Paris couldn't find the strength to get in her car and go the extra miles to pick up Frenchie. Instead, once Ronnie dropped her off, she got her suitcase inside her kitchen door, stripped off her clothes, donned her favorite comfy nightgown, flopped onto her bed, and fell into a deep sleep. Twelve hours later, Paris opened her eyes and smiled. Dragging herself from sleep, she made her typical strong coffee and padded to the computer. The silence reminded her she needed to call her oldest son and retrieve Frenchie. Once the screen came on, Paris gave herself over to relating her weekend.

> **While chatting in the Gazebo, I think one time I mentioned that as a child I had never been to a bunking party, and that is something I had missed. Then the talk began for a slumber party in Texas. Someone, I am sure it was one of the guys, Ducky I think said, AYE a nekkid pajama party. So we all got to kidding about that. I just wonder how**

many of the non-chat regulars who were coming and going in there thought we were really going to do that? LOL. Well Friday, my sister and I arrived in the late afternoon, after 6 PM. at the Motel 6 in Garland, Texas. It was close to where Nancy lived. When we were checking in I saw Yellow Duck coming towards us. I hugged his neck then got him to help us carry up our bags. Nancy had reserved 4 rooms in a row. My sister and I were on the end and then Nancy and Belle... They decided to just stay there to be near the fun. Next was Deborahsu's room. The guys Duck and Fooled shared the other room. The first night, we went to a neat place in Dallas and had supper and played pool! The food was great and we had a fun time playing pool. We then went to a comedy club where they did ad-libs. It was hilarious!

After that we all got comfortable and all 6 of us, plus Belle's little silky dog piled up on 2 beds in one room (with the door open, Lol) and talked, told jokes, and giggled and ate snacks! We finally parted for the night and got some sleep. I told them that I would kiss someone's azz on Broadway Street if one of them would bring me some coffee the next morning. Next morning, Ducky had placed a cup in front of our door and Belle brought me a big mug and my sister got me some~ sooooooo~ Then we were off to the luncheon! We took 2 cars. Nancy

was in the lead car. We followed. (Well, my
sister did not attend any of the functions,
as she just wanted solitude after the hectic
year she had been having) We left an hour
before the luncheon started. Somehow! We
got lost! And we were about 45 minutes
late! Well, we made it and I really enjoyed
meeting so many wonderful folks that I
have been chatting with for nearly a year!
I don't dare start naming names for fear of
leaving out a name, but you know who you
are! Just LOVELY, LOVELY people! We all
sat out by the pool and visited for an hour
or so. That night we went to the West End
and went to the Froggy Bottoms, which
was a Karaoke club. The first I have ever
been to. We strolled all around looking at
many different places. We ended up eating
a breakfast type meal at the Waffle house
for supper! We then all went back and piled
on the beds with our snacks that Deb had
gotten for us. Oreos, chips and dips and
nuts! We laughed and laughed. As some of
you may remember, I have never gotten to
just be a kid or a teen. These good times that
I am having lately with my new friends are
the nearest thing to that I have ever had.
This must be what it must be like to live in
a dorm and just have FUN! My sister was so
happy to see me having fun with my friends
like she and her friends have always had! I
hated to leave them all, but some had to leave
early Sunday morning. My friend Gaye38

called and my sister and I met with her, her husband Ray and Susie444 from the UK, at Bennigan's for lunch after we checked out. The other friends were not able to make it as they had scattered by then. What delightful people they are and my sister was in on this visit! We said our goodbyes and hope to see as many as possible at the Arkansas Mini Bash on July 15Th in Hot Spring Arkansas! Hope you all can join us for the fun! Love, Paris - Texas Luncheon

Paris posted her latest blog and rolled back in her chair. Deciding to go back to bed for a few hours, she yawned and slowly made her way there.

The next day, Paris received a surprise visit from Gary. He had brought Frenchie back, so Paris didn't have to get out. Sharing a good chat before he left for work, he assured her that Chuck had not minded dog-sitting, and neither had April, his wife. Following them to the kitchen door as they said their good-byes, Frenchie scratched, barked, and ran around in impatient circle, demanding Paris's attention. Paris, always worried that Frenchie would run out, picked him up, closed the door quickly, and made her way to the media room. As she settled on the sofa, she tucked her feet under a blanket. Frenchie rooted around to make a comfortable place in her lap. Paris scratched his ears and started talking to him as though he could really understand.

"Oh, Frenchie, I can hardly believe it. I had such a great time. It seemed like I've known this group forever! Mr. Right wasn't there, but maybe a Mr. In-Between. More than that, I finally understand why my sister always enjoyed her friends and sleepovers."

Leaning over, she lowered her voice to a stage whisper and

continued in Frenchie's ear. "Personally, I had wondered if she and her friends weren't queer."

Returning to her former upright position, she reminisced, "But, after popcorn, movies, and giggling with the girls, my new friends disclosed hang-ups and insecurities, just like I have. And, listen to this, Frenchie: they do outrageous and sometimes naughty things! Well, it's just so liberating. I can't imagine why I haven't taken the chance on friendships before. Oh, yeah— Mother. Well, no more! Maybe I truly am a late, make that a very late, bloomer. Guess that makes me a baby-boomer bloomer!" She giggled. "I've never felt like this. Ronnie and I even seemed closer than ever on the way home. Perhaps I need to cut her some slack. What do you think? She's really not the prude I thought. Know what, Frenchie? Sometimes I think she likes me." Leaning back over Frenchie's ear, she whispered, "And some of the time I like her."

Frenchie's head dipped from side to side, just like he was listening. Then he stretched up to lick the tears on Paris's cheeks.

"Come on, boy. I'll get your food. I feel like eating a jar of dill pickles and maybe fixin' a hot dog with chili. Did I tell you how Ronnie tried her best not to be embarrassed when I told her I'd been designated the SFF 'official pecker checker'?" Paris laughed so hard that more tears came to her eyes. "I had so much fun with that!"

Chapter 7

"Stage 4!" Paris's eyes flew open, and she sat straight up. Startled but strangely unafraid, a warm, peaceful feeling washed over her. What a strange dream! Shaking off the last bit of slumber, Paris shifted to the edge of the bed. Her day would be filled with so many things to do, she'd better get started.

Paris was going out to Ronnie's house to spend the night. It was so nice to actually have a sisterly relationship. Ever since the Texas trip a couple of months ago, they had enjoyed one another. Life was not so bad with a few friends and a sister. In fact, that was the topic of last night's blog.

I Choose To be Happy For the Rest of My Life

Happiness, I have found after all these 63 years is a true choice! We can choose to focus on our past hurts, slights, wrongs or we can choose to move forward, forward, forgive and forget. Sounds very simple doesn't it! IT TRULY IS! I lived for years

with hurts. I was a narcissistic scorekeeper. You would not even know me. I hope to God, that old me is DEAD! At least the negative traits. That never got me happiness. Then I thought that someday when I became rich, or found Prince Charming that I would reach happiness! How many precious years I wasted!

Happiness is made of many small things, small moments, small kindnesses. If we simply choose to ignore the small inconveniences, the pettiness of others, and look only for the good in folks and reflect that good with our kindness and our smiles and our love. We will soon be filled to the brim with happiness! At least it has worked for me; you might give it a try!

Paris gathered clothes, shoes, jewelry, etc. to haul to Ronnie's. Yep, she was off again. Not too bad for a recent recluse with nowhere to go and no one to do it with. Paris had collected way more than she needed, but she and Ronnie would go through and pick out what to pack for the St. Petersburg International Bloggers' Bash. Bloggers from all over the world were coming. It was so exciting! Paris still could hardly believe that Ronnie had told her that she needed to go. No lectures, no preaching, just, "Paris, you need to go, and I will get you there." Ronnie had arranged for Paris to fly out of Memphis and provided her with a loaded Visa card so she'd have money while she was there. Ronnie had explained that she was going to Nashville to see her youngest daughter, the country singer, and her two grandsons anyway, so she'd take Paris to the Memphis airport and pick her up on the way back. It was all planned. Everything was very exciting, but Paris was also a little apprehensive. She was traveling alone, and she really hadn't been feeling all that well.

"Pull it together, girl. You're just letting ol' Murphy ruin your life again."

Determined nothing would rob her of this treat, Paris lugged load after load of wardrobe possibilities to her trusty blue Grand Am. True, the Grand Am was a come down from her dream car, a pearl Caddy, but it got her from point A to point B—at least most of the time.

"Right now, nothing could be bad, 'cause Paris is headed to the bash!" Paris smiled. Car stuffed, she put the rhinestone-studded leash on Frenchie, locked the kitchen door, and squeezed behind the wheel. "I'll miss you, Frenchie, my angel dog, but you'll enjoy the weekend with Chuck again." Reassuring the dog with an extra love pat and shoving him into the back seat, Paris backed down the driveway and started on her next great adventure.

Later in the afternoon, Paris and Ronnie sat on the floor, surrounded by the mounds of clothes. Paris had put each outfit together with matching shoes and accessories while Ronnie was rolling them to demonstrate the most efficient way to get too much in the too-small suitcase. Panties and hose were rolled and stuffed into shoes.

Ronnie held up an item and said, "Now, why do you need this?"

Paris laughed and giggled like a little girl. "It's absolutely necessary to complete the outfit. Don't you know anything about fashion? Besides, I have a certain image to maintain now that I'm famous—or infamous."

Ronnie shook her head and sighed. She rolled each blouse, pant, or dress, and then carefully placed each in the suitcase.

"This pair looks new," Ronnie observed with a raised eyebrow.

Looking somewhat embarrassed, Paris said, "Well, I've been losing a little weight lately, so I went to Kmart and bought two pairs of pants. You're not mad, are you?"

"Naw, I'm proud of you losing some weight. St. Pete Bash must be a strong motivator. If you keep it up, you might not need to take all those medications you take."

"Actually, I have stopped several or halved the amounts I take. Mostly due to not having the money, but I seem to be doing much better. Just a little tired."

"It helps to have plans for fun. Now, let's check to make sure we have everything you need." They made a list of missing items, and the sisters piled into Ronnie's dark-blue Maxima for a Wal-Mart run.

On the way, Paris thought about the voice that had awakened her. It wasn't the same whiney voice she heard a year ago when she was so depressed. It was strong voice, yet not threatening. Was it a dream? Then she remembered another time when a voice talked to her—not Murphy's but a deep, authoritative voice. "Did you ever read the blog I wrote about the Fulcrum?" Paris asked Ronnie.

"No, I've never been on your blogs. I'm still not sure how I feel about all this chatting and writing to strangers." Ronnie glanced over to Paris and then continued, "Never mind. Tell me about the Fulcrum."

Paris brightened and launched into telling Ronnie how, many years ago, a very religious former coworker had stopped by to see her at home. "I was getting ready to leave the next day after work to visit the in-laws."

"What does that have to do with a fulcrum?" Ronnie broke in impatiently.

"Well …"

> The night before I was to leave the next day, she prayed for me the regular way, then in "tongues." NOW PARDON ME FOR what I am about to say, I am thinking to myself that is nice that she is praying for me. But it all sounds like gobbledygook to me. I thought to myself, Now, God, if you are listening, how about something just for me, a sign of some kind? At that very instance, she started speaking in French! I still could not understand a word of it, but if there were two people in a room and one was speaking Arabic, and one was speaking French, I think that you could tell the difference. And God knows, I do have a love for French things! It was probable less than 20 minutes after that, a word popped into my head. A word that I had never heard. It kept repeating over and over like a song sometimes will do. It kept on, and on…Finally I ask her, "Do you know what FULCRUM means?" Well she had heard it, but did not remember what it meant. So we looked it up. A: the support about which a lever turns B: one that supplies capability for action. She said it was kind of like an axle that turns a wheel. I said, "Why do you think it keeps going around in my head like that?" She said that she thought maybe God was trying to tell

me that I was the center holding my family together or something like that. Well the next day we had a hug and a prayer for a safe trip and of course to keep the kids safe. On the drive home, no matter how loud I played the radio that word kept repeating in my head! I got home and had to go to work. The next day, I got a call, but they asked for someone else first. The storeowner's wife who was now my friend took me into the break room and said to sit down and take a deep breath. She said the call was to let me know that a truck had run into the house but my boys were all right. She was to drive me home. Another followed her driving my car so I knew it must be bad. When I arrived, there were police, a crowd of neighbors, etc. We lived on a curve of a well-traveled street. There was a lot of construction going on past our house. A truck had NOT actually run into the house. An empty dump truck was speeding and as it rounded the curve, an axle broke. The tire and wheel came loose and started bouncing. It bounced up and over a cedar tree, and took out the top. It hit the ground, took another bounce and hit the corner of our brick house just inches away from the 6 foot long window on the front of the house. The police said it was a miracle that it didn't go right through the window because it had hit the house with such force that it broke the bricks and cracked the sheetrock on the wall inside and pictures

fell off the wall. The force moved the table and knocked over a chair! I found out that just minutes before it hit, the boys had gone in the kitchen to raid the refrigerator. They had been sitting at the dining table in front of the window finishing their homework! Fulcrum, Fulcrum, Fulcrum ... Warning from God?

"Oh, Paris," exclaimed Ronnie, "you are so bizarre and dramatic! Where did that come from?" Ronnie glanced at her and then added, "It does seem rather prophetic yet farfetched! Come on, though, and quit being a goose. We're here, and we have shopping to do. I think I'm as excited as you are that you're going. Let's go get the things you need."

As the sisters walked into Wal-Mart, the store photographer greeted them and handed them a coupon for a free eight-by-ten photo. Paris turned to Ronnie and confided, "You know, I haven't had a professional picture taken in more than ten years."

"Let's do it, then. I'll pay. You know it won't be really free," Ronnie responded.

After several reassurances that Paris looked beautiful—both from the photographer and from Ronnie—Paris agreed. They moved to the portrait studio, discussed package options, and selected a background. Each took her appropriate place. Paris was seated on the stool. The photographer moved around, checking the lighting, and then settled behind the camera. Ronnie took her spot behind the photographer to better coach. Clucking like a mother hen, she encouraged Paris to relax and smile.

"Smile! Let's see some teeth!" the photographer cajoled.

"You know why I hate to smile with my teeth showing don't you?" Paris asked Ronnie as the photographer was rearranging her equipment.

"No, why?"

"You really should read my blogs! I used the reason as another blog topic."

> **I think the real reason I don't show my teeth more when I smile, is because of my father! When we first got our Television set, he kept going on about Martha Ray and what a big, awful mouth she had. He was talking to my momma, but I felt embarrassed for some reason. It is very important for men as Dads and Grandfathers to be aware that there could be little sensitive ears listening to your remarks about women. Little girls want to please you and might take it wrong, like I did!**

"How absurd!" the photographer stated adamantly.

"Incredible! How could you make something personal out of that? You have a beautiful smile!" Ronnie added.

"Well, if you really think so. I do think my hair looks good, and I would love to have a picture!" Paris smiled, and the pictures were snapped.

Told to return in thirty minutes to look at the proofs, the sisters proceeded to meander through the store. Of course, they checked out the clothing section, just to make sure there wasn't something Paris might need. Ronnie would grab something and hold it up to Paris and then move back to evaluate.

"Nope. That doesn't work."

"What about this?" Paris asked, picking up a soft, green, sparkly shirt.

"Better. But do you really need it?"

"A better question is, where would we put it? My one little suitcase is nearly exploding as it is!" Paris countered.

The sisters had a good laugh and got back to searching for the specific items on their list. Soon the basket was filled, and they headed to the checkout stand. While waiting in line, they tossed in hand sanitizer and gum for the flight. Scanning each item, the friendly cashier began asking the usual questions. Paris began to feel the familiar panic rise as the cashier came closer to the end of the purchases.

"Ronnie, should we put some of this back? Maybe I don't really need these things. I could …"

"You're being a goose again! You do need them, and I wouldn't do this if I couldn't afford it or didn't want to, so quit your worrying."

"I know, but you are already paying for the trip and the Visa card, and …"

"Paris! If you go on a trip, you have to do it right. Now let me get this paid for, and let's go look at those pictures."

When they got to the photo shop, they were shown to a computer and told how to navigate the photo selections. "These are great! You look so pretty with that smile. I envy your perfect teeth," said Ronnie. "No rabbit teeth like me."

"They really are good, aren't they?" Paris pondered as she clicked on each. "I like this one best." She selected a close head shot showing off her turquoise sweater, wavy shoulder-length blonde hair, and a beautiful toothy smile. "It would make a great obit picture!" Paris declared.

The photographer, who had finished with another customer and had come to stand close to the sisters, made a choking sound and cut her eyes to Ronnie.

"Paris, don't even jest about such a thing! Ronnie protested.

"You've never even really been sick. I know you've thought you've had this and that, but it's been mostly in your head. The things you take medicine for are caused by you being overweight. Maybe when you lose a few more pounds, you won't even need your medicines."

"I'm just sayin'. You know I don't have a problem with stuff like that. I sold those prearrangements for years. I don't even mind being around dead bodies. Remember, I did Mom's hair and makeup when she died."

"You are so weird!" Ronnie declared, rolling her eyes again.

Paris smiled as she realized she didn't take offense at Ronnie's comment. They seemed to be bantering like real sisters.

As they were driving back to Ronnie's home, Paris hesitantly asked, "Did I tell you about my dream last night? Well, technically this morning and not actually a dream. More like a voice."

"Nooo, what did this voice say?"

Paris could hear the skepticism laced in Ronnie's voice and thought to herself, *I can get upset, mad, and sull-up like I used to, or I can be positive and go for it, trusting it will turn out okay and she will not make fun of me.*

"It was a loud, deep man's voice that said 'Stage 4.'"

"Is that the reason you said that about the obit picture? Oh, Paris, surely you don't believe that …" Ronnie's voice trailed off, but her thoughts continued, *Here she goes again. Last year she just knew she had diabetes. The year before it was fibromyalgia. Before that it was Parkinson's as well as PTSD. It's always some awful, dreaded disease, some catastrophe that needs money, or some wild plan to catch a man! Will she ever change? Deep breath! Try to be nice now, Ronnie, and don't ruin things.* Taking another deep, calming breath, Ronnie continued aloud, "Did it scare you?"

"No, in fact, I felt warm and peaceful—even loved," Paris responded.

Ronnie hadn't expected that answer. She expected something more dramatic and Murphyish. "I do believe that the Lord can speak to us," Ronnie said quietly.

Paris realized that Ronnie believed her. Actually, Paris wasn't sure it was the Lord who spoke to her, but she believed in covering all her bases. She had studied and dabbled in most everything: Buddhism, Judaism, Mormonism, even astrology. She read horoscopes, consulted psychic readers, and had her charts and moon phases read. But deep in her heart, she clung to her early beliefs in Jesus Christ as her Lord and Savior. She also knew her "voice" spoke with authority and brought a peacefulness, rather than panic, over the implications. Yes, if she were a betting person, she'd say it was God's voice.

These thoughts were much too heavy, especially when she had a trip planned and people to see. So, Paris's old mantra of "I'll think about it tomorrow" from *Gone with the Wind* helped her to put the voice on the back burner. She refused to think about it again until after the St. Petersburg Bash. Maybe she'd find Mr. Right—rich, handsome, available. She would much rather think about the possibilities.

It was a perfect ending to an impromptu evening of dinner and dancing with a mysterious gentleman who had caught her eye. He was very handsome, with his gorgeous head of white hair, great tan, and come-hither smile. Walking barefoot on the beach, hand in hand, under a full moon was so romantic! They stopped in companionable silence to listen to the waves lapping at the shore. Slowly, he drew her into his arms. His lips closed possessively on hers, while his hands began to roam.

"Paris," Ronnie interrupted, "we're here. Let's get this stuff packed and us ready for bed. Remember, we need to get up early if we're going to make the plane. Do you need anything else?"

"No, I'm good," Paris replied dreamily. "I doubt I can sleep.

I'm so excited!" Paris smiled to herself, knowing that Ronnie would be embarrassed if she knew exactly what would be keeping her up and excited. But, oh, later she would sleep and dream.

The next morning was a blur. Paris was not used to this early rising and get going stuff. Ronnie had all but shoved Paris in the car, fussing that the plane would leave her if she didn't hurry up. The trip to Memphis was uneventful but pleasant. Each sister was very sleepy, yet wanting to make their time together count, so they both made an effort to talk.

"Tell me more about your blog friends," Ronnie asked.

"You're sure? I could go on for hours. They come from all walks of life, live all over the world, and are just so nice and supportive! In fact, I credit them for the healing of my poor wounded heart and from feeling so misunderstood and rejected for most of my life," Paris gushed.

"Wow. Maybe a little too much for this early in the morning. If I didn't know better, I would think you were talking about a new love, rather than friends on a dating site."

"You still don't get it, do you? But why a love?"

"When you have a new love, you say nice things about them. You want to spend all your time with them. You glow and gush. Pretty much like you just did."

"Don't forget I like to be a little naughty with a lover." Paris broke into a mischievous smile.

"I said love, not lover. La, la, la!" Ronnie countered.

The two and a half hours had flown by, and Ronnie pulled into the short-term parking lot. After quickly finding a spot, she popped the trunk, hopped out of the car, heaved out the luggage, and checked the car for missing items. By this time, Paris had finally exited the car and was hurrying to catch up with Ronnie. Both sisters were huffing and puffing by the time they entered the airport. Once Ronnie got Paris checked in and the suitcase tagged, weighed, and on the conveyer, she suggested that they eat some breakfast until it was time for Paris to board.

"If they have strong, hot, black coffee, I'm in!"

As they were walking to the boarding area after their hurried breakfast and coffee, Ronnie repeated to Paris all the dos and don'ts of traveling and being in a strange town, hotel, etc.

Teasingly, Paris replied, "What? Do you think I'm one of your girls? I've flown a time or two. Or is it that you care?"

Hesitantly, Ronnie put her arms around Paris and replied, "Well, I've never had a real sister to worry about before. Now, hurry up before you miss your plane."

Chapter 8

The weekend passed quickly, and Ronnie returned to Memphis to pick up Paris. She parked her well-traveled Maxima in short-term and hurried into the terminal as far as security allowed. Although she was just a few minutes late, most of the passengers had already deplaned. There were couples hugging, children running around their wearied parents, singles looking around for flight connection information, but no Paris. Ronnie was becoming increasingly more anxious as the minutes ticked by and the area cleared out. She moved around to see if she could get a better look down the now-empty hallway.

"It would be just like her to miss her plane! She probably overslept. What am I going to do?" Ronnie muttered as she flagged down a Delta attendant.

"May I help you with something?" the stranger asked.

"Yes. My sister was supposed to arrive. Sorry, never mind. I here she comes," Ronnie responded apologetically as she saw Paris being pushed in a wheelchair up the ramp toward the exit.

Paris waved and called out, "How do you like my wheels? Beats walking!"

Ronnie gave her a tight little welcoming smile, swallowed

her questions, and grabbed the luggage, all the while wondering what illness or scheme her sister had concocted this time. "Let's go. It will be dark before we get home."

Soon they were in the car, speeding toward Little Rock. Paris regaled Ronnie with the details of the St. Petersburg Bash, droning on about who she talked to, what she wore, how she was going to write her blogs. Finally, Ronnie couldn't wait anymore. "What's up with the wheelchair bit?"

"I've just been so tired lately, and the nicest young man asked if I wanted a ride. Did you know for only five dollars, you can have someone push you in a wheelchair from one plane to another? You don't have to worry about finding anything, because they take care of everything. You feel so pampered and special!"

Ronnie rolled her eyes and made a little disapproving huff sound. *How lazy can one person be?* Looking over at Paris, she realized that Paris had dropped off to sleep. Probably a good thing. She really didn't want to spoil Paris's trip with thoughtless words best left unspoken. "Probably too much partying," she muttered under her breath.

Ronnie pulled up the steep Berkshire driveway and put the car in park. Not much longer and she would be home with her sweet husband, sanity, and quiet. All she had to do was get the luggage out and Paris out, and she'd be on her way. Hurriedly, she deposited the suitcase on the steps, gave Paris a quick hug, and hopped back in the car. Just as Paris opened her kitchen door, she turned and indicated to Ronnie that she should roll down the window.

"Do you think my eyes are jaundiced?"

Here we go again. Ronnie rolled her eyes (something she found herself doing a lot these days) and bit back a sharp retort. "I really can't see in this light, but I haven't noticed them being unusual.

Why do you even think? Never mind." Ronnie reminded herself of their new sisterly relationship. "Let me look in the light."

Getting back out of the car, she followed Paris into the house. Under the kitchen light, Ronnie looked at Paris's eyes. "Well, they do look a little yellow. Maybe you should call a doctor tomorrow, just to be on the safe side."

After almost twenty-four hours of sleep, Paris dragged herself out of bed and made it to her bathroom. She flipped on the mirror light switch, pried her eyes open, and peered into the mirror. Yep, still yellow. Paris gave a very typical French shrug and continued with daily rituals. More awake now, she shuffled down the hallway and put her coffee on. Turning to let Frenchie out, she remembered she still hadn't picked him up. She glanced at the clock and decided it was not too late to call Gary and make arrangements to get Frenchie. After all, he was a night owl too.

Replacing the phone, she poured her coffee and made her way to her computer. She couldn't wait to post about her St. Petersburg Bash experience.

> **Some of you have asked for a blow by blow,
> including what I wore! I will do my best.
> Men, please bear with me! I got to my
> sister's house late about 9pm Tuesday. I had
> dropped Lil' Frenchie off at my son's house.
> He lives near there. I had been preparing for
> almost a week but seems that I still am so
> slow and put everything off until the last.
> The packing and lugging the suitcase, etc.
> was almost more than I could handle. When
> I finally made it to my sister's driveway and
> parked, I put my head down for a minute**

in utter relief! I knew she would handle things from then on! We tried to sleep until 3:20 am and we were off to Memphis at 3:30 am. When we left Little Rock, it was raining and cold. I chose to wear a charcoal gray velvet sweat suit with a lighter almost steel/blue gray cotton knit top that had a portrait neckline and three buttons that were rhinestones. I wore espadrilles that were charcoal, the lighter charcoal blue and black with rope type wedges and black ties. Since it was cold, I wore black socks. My purse was black cloth. We had a lovely talk and visit on the way. We ate a breakfast meal at the airport then she saw me to the security check in area and waved to me. I boarded the flight and looked for my seat. I found I was sitting next to a handsome young man that I had made eye contact in the waiting area of the airport. We had a pleasant conversation. It turned out he worked on Airplane wheels! So he was an old hand at flying and the routine. I relaxed a bit and figured I could just watch him if anything went wrong. I called him my first angel. He smiled sweetly. He noticed I was very nervous. I confided that I had not flown in about 15 years and never alone. He said what makes you nervous? I said the takeoff, because they go so fast and I cannot see where they are going and I don't have a hand to hold like I always have had before. Upon take off, he reached across and held my hand until we were safely in the air. He got my bag out of the overhead compartment and walked me to the tram and showed me where I boarded the Super Shuttle that my sister had arranged. There were a group of women on it who were all so pleasant and friendly! They were dialysis therapists. I had a very pleasant trip to the hotel. When I arrived, Fossil Fetcher came out and greeted me with a big hug, L. was inside at the check in table. I saw many friends. I excused myself to go to the room. I freshened up and changed to something more suitable to the afternoon sunny mild weather in Florida. I chose to wear, navy cuffed, cropped pants with a short-sleeved navy top with nautical appliqués of a gold star and other gold and white touches with silver studs, I wore gold platform mules and I carried a navy clutch purse. I went on the covered porch that overlooked the ocean and pool area. I visited and met so many wonderful folks and then I went to supper and turned in early because I was so exhausted! More tomorrow! Love, Paris

St. Pete Friday

My roommate woke me at 1:30. Some of my friends had been asking about me. I was exhausted from my arrival the day before. I dressed for the day in teal linen pants with a matching teal with white horizontal stripe matching cotton knit shirt. It had a nautical logo embroidered on it. I wore silver wide hoop earrings and fixed my hair up in a ponytail with it fluffed a bit. I wore a little silly teal fufu around it that had points of organza fabric on it. For my shoes, I had straw three-inch heels. They had teal flowers of straw. They were the cute kind that you could not help but jiggle and wiggle a bit as you walk! I went down and joined the group for visiting overlooking the pool. We later went to the grocery store across the street. I got fresh fruit, bottled spring water, buttermilk and cheese and crackers. I got to meet and visit with so many fine folks. I don't want to start naming names for fear I might omit someone. Let's just say that I think I ended up meeting and chatting with almost all who were there at some point in the three days. There was not one who was not a delight! The facilities were very conducive to casual chatting and visiting. Very relaxing and the scenery was beautiful! I went back to my room to prepare for the Karaoke Night. For that evening, I chose something that was not too dressy because it was not a dress event and I realized many were going casual. I chose a pair of black cotton knit slacks and a Black top that had a deep V-neck but had almost like spaghetti strap criss crosses in the V. It was fitted under the bust. And slightly flared. I also added a soft black swing jacket of a lightweight knit fabric. I wore black and gold earrings and carried a black tapestry clutch bag. I chose about three inch black fabric heels. I had dinner at the hotel with two of my dear couple friends. Then it was time for Karaoke! (No, I did not, and do not SING! The place would have emptied like a fire drill if I had!) I went in the bar; everyone was having a wonderful time! I visited with this one and that one! Of course the highlight was getting to visit with Loth again, and meet his Em. Quite a few of his "other wives" were there, I think I was # 12! Em just laughs, what a good sport! The evening was going so well, AND THEN, I look across to the end of the bar and see this drop dead handsome guy who looks like Richard Gere! He walked towards me and said, "I told you I would be here." He had asked for a dance and told me he would buy me a drink! (I had chatted with him in the SFF Chat rooms) I had a frozen margarita and then he chose a song and gave the man a tip to play it. He looked into my eyes and sang it to me and gently kissed my hand. I felt like "swoooooooooning" Here is the song: *Wonderful Tonight* by Eric Clapton, just close your eyes and share this memory with me. I will always remember this Dance! Now let me say, He also danced with a friend of mine. He picked out a song for her, also and I think he sang it to her. But, still...

Anyway, he said he was going to Boston on a 6am flight and had not eaten lunch or dinner and asked if would we walk across the street to breakfast at Bennigan's with him. We said we weren't very hungry but we would keep him company. As we started across the 4 lane street in front of the hotel, it began a soft gentle, warm rain. Just as we got in the middle of the street, the wind started to blow and the bottom fell out in a deluge. By the time we got all the way across the street, we looked like drowned rats and were soaked to our underwear! We struggled into Bennigan's and they said they had stopped serving. It was 12 AM but they handed us big stacks of dinner napkins to sop off with. The poor fellow felt bad that he had talked us into this when he could have gotten the car, so he ran back across the street in the pouring rain to get the car. He did not want to settle for breakfast at the Waffle House. He wanted a nicer place. After about 15 minutes of driving around looking for a place that was open, that is just where we ended up! I had the pecan waffle after my friend agreed to eat some of it. We had as good a visit as 3 sopping wet people could have! We went back to the hotel and visited a bit in the lobby. My friend excused herself to go to bed, as it was quite late by then. I asked the gentleman if he would walk me to my elevator, as it was outside and thru some more doors. He did and then he rode up to the room with me. He did not crowd me. He said he would call me when he came through Little Rock. We shared a little damp hug. - Thanks for sharing my memories! Love, Paris

St. Petersburg Saturday:

I was very tired and weak, did not know why. I rested in my room and ate the rest of the fruit and some crackers and cheese that I had gotten at the grocery store across the street. I had buttermilk and chicken broth. I did some "beauty treatments" facial masque, etc. I showered and pin curled my hair, I was hoping to wear it down like in the picture on my profile. I blew it dry instead of letting it dry overnight. When I took it down it did not do right. I was shocked to see that it was almost 4 p.m. I put on blue-grey cotton knit outfit. The pants and shirt were the same color but there was a white inset in the deep V-neck. I wore blue mules. I went down to the patio area that overlooks the pool and beach to visit for about an hour. I then returned to my room to get dressed for the big event, The Mardi Gras Ball! I wore a dress that I had bought in the early 1990's when my Lil' Hubby and I went on a cruise. It was last worn by my dear mother at my parents' 50th wedding anniversary! I removed the gigantic shoulder pads! LOL.

It was a sheath dress that came below the knee. It had a high neck and elbow length sleeves. The sleeves were wide and had long peaks. It was black with gold sequins. The design of the sequins was such that it drew attention upwards toward the face. I wore opaque black pantyhose and black velvet high heels. I carried a black velvet evening clutch bag with rhinestones. I wore my hair up in a Classic French Twist! I wore antique earrings from my mother that my sister loaned me. They were gold with rhinestone balls that dangled. (Very ELEGANT! Ooh La La ! lol) Now for the biggie.

I suffer from anxiety and had almost become a recluse. I leave my house only 3 or 4 times a month. I have never attended a big function like this unescorted. Even with someone, I would have spent most of the time hiding out in the restroom! I gave not a thought to this, and entered the Banquet/Ballroom with almost a hundred folks there, all by myself! I flitted from table to table hugging and visiting with everyone like we were all relatives and this was old home week! I was not one bit nervous! YOU CAN NOT IMAGINE what a big miracle this is! This would have been totally inconceivable, before joining SFF! Anyway, I sat with my dear friends, D. and her quiet fiancée, R. who turned out to be the life of the party when he excused himself and came back in dressed as CUPID! I also sat with my dear friend A. that I finally got to meet this trip and her friend, HawkSlayer. I got up and asked several men to dance and some asked me! I even danced with a tall floozy flapper! The old me would have been mortified and afraid of what everyone would think! I felt such a sense of freedom and joy!

One handsome older man came up to me and confided that he had been trying to get my attention. He said he had asked me to join him the other day across the street with some friends who were going to get lunch but I sort of blew him off and said I was eating at the hotel with friends. I didn't even remember! I said "Well I thought you were with someone." He said he was just sitting with someone. He wanted to get to know me. The party continued down stairs in the Karaoke bar after the ball. The darling man asked me if I wanted a drink and I said I would love some ice water! He bought a coke and got some ice water. He later asked if I wanted the coke. He said he did not really want it…. I understood immediately!

I said, "OHHH you only bought it because you did not want to ask for free ice water!" He smiled! He asked me if I would like to go for a walk and to talk. I said that I would love to. We walked out and all around the pool and then found a spot at the almost dark Tiki outside bar. We sat and talked for a long time. I finally saw the longing in his eyes and asked if he would like a kiss! He said he had wanted one since he first saw me! We shared some sweet tender kisses and talked more. He lived in Florida. He is not a blogger or does not chat much. I had checked him out at the ball with some who knew him. They said he was not a player but a very nice sincere man. He invited me to change my flight and stay a week. Then he asked me to think about wintering in Fla. with him! Very Tempting! Somewhere in the conversation, I told him of Lil' Frenchie! He said he was at a place in his life where he did not want the responsibility of an animal. He liked them, but if he wanted to pick up and go, he wanted to be able to do that! He was a lovely man, but Love ME, Love Lil' Frenchie! Hoped you enjoyed sharing more of my wonderful memories! Hugs, Paris Returning Home:

I got up, got around and got my shower and got dressed. I wore black cotton knit pants, black "V" neck cotton tee shirt trimmed with brown beads. I had a vest that was black, brown and gold animal print. I wore my special ivory wide bracelet from India, it is made from trimmings from the tusks, it has a large amber stone in the center. I wore black flats. I had my hair pulled back in a fluffy ponytail and tied with black and gold velvet strips. I packed and checked out. I put my bags in the hospitality room. I then went to a late breakfast at the hotel. I went around and said my goodbyes. I called the shuttle service and had them come an hour earlier so I would not have to rush as much and would be sure to catch my flight. I went outside and said goodbye to the folks on the patio area and took another good look around at the lovely facilities and the magnificent scenery! I caught the shuttle and had a delightful lady to talk with. She had been there giving a lecture to some UPS folks on some software. I loved the tropical scenes, looked like a whole different country from Arkansas! I got to the Airport in plenty of time. I had a sandwich at the food court and went to the gate. When I boarded the plane and found my seat, I found I was sitting between two ladies who were much more "fluffy" than me! I thought I would be claustrophobic, the plane was totally full! But, I found I felt strangely comforted! The lady on the aisle seat was a joy to talk with. She owned her own business and went around instructing math teachers on innovative teaching methods. She and her husband had a sailboat down on some island. I shared with her the story of my "angel" who held my hand on takeoff when I was frightened. As we took off, she reached over and held my hand like a mother holding a little kid's hand! I arrived in the Memphis Airport and was greeted by the smiling face of my dear sister! We got my bags and headed home! Thanks for sharing my memories of my great adventure! My dear Friends! Hugs, Paris

Chapter 9

It had totally exhausted Paris to post her great adventures at the St. Pete Bash, so she didn't drag herself from bed until a little past noon. She shuffled down the hall to the kitchen, put the coffee on, sat down in her favorite Queen Anne chair, and realized how much she missed Li'l Frenchie's companionship. *I must have jet lag. I'm exhausted, and I haven't done anything yet! As much as I love Frenchie, I don't know if I have the energy to let him out and in.*

The empty house had no answer.

Paris pushed her body up to go get the coffee that was now ready. *Maybe this will get me going.* Coffee in hand, Paris made her way to the bathroom. "Hmmm …" Paris muttered as she looked at strange-colored poopie. After washing her hands, she examined her eyes. Definitely jaundiced! Next, she made her way to the computer and googled: clay poopie, orange pee, and jaundiced eyes. She read the information supplied by WebMD.

"Definitely not good! I'd better find a doctor." Paris returned to the kitchen to get her phone book and searched for an appropriate doctor. Saying a quick prayer, she picked up the phone and dialed.

Returning from the doctor's office two days later, Paris pulled into the carport and rested her head on the steering wheel. *Well, that seemed okay,* she thought. *Just a few questions, a few little tests; nothing to worry about. At least I know now that the jaundice is causing all this itching.* Paris got out of the car. She could hear Frenchie barking and scratching at the kitchen door for all he was worth.

Carefully opening the door, she scooped Frenchie up and asked, "Are you worried about me, fellow? I'm so glad you're back! The house was so quiet and empty without you. Don't you worry about me. Here, now, let's let you run outside for a while." After letting Frenchie out and back in again, Paris went to her media room and flipped on the TV. Curling up comfortably on the couch, she closed her eyes.

The shrill ring of the phone awakened her. Listening carefully, she shuffled through papers on the coffee table to find a pen and something to write on. She wrote down a date, time, and place. Taking a deep breath, Paris made her way her computer and logged on to post:

May I Ask

The Doctor's office called me back today and said they did not want to wait till Monday for me to have the MRI on my Liver, Spleen, and kidney area. I am scheduled for 10:30 tomorrow. I go see the doctor at 2:00. If it is a blocked bile duct, they want to do the procedure MONDAY! I hope that is all there is to it. The nurse said that they might be able to do it on an outpatient basis. I am a bit frightened! - Hugs, Paris

11/03/06   Dear Friends, Health Update

First of all thanks to all of you for your supportive comments, prayers and good wishes! The doctor told me today that evidently where the two ducts from my liver come together, scar tissue from the removal of my gallbladder has formed and blocked it. The bile has backed up. It has caused the jaundice. He explained that he could do a procedure by going down thru my throat and can put in a stent (a straw like thing they sometimes use in hearts) to hold open the drainage hole. He said the relief and feeling better should happen almost immediately! He saw no tumors or growths. THANK GOD! I was so afraid it might be the big "C". I was so grateful for this good news; I came home and fell into a very peaceful deep sleep! It was the first in a while! Thanks to all of you, My DEAR FRIENDS! - Hugs, Paris

— Chapter 10 —

The outpatient procedure to put in the stent had gone well once it got started. Typically, it started late and took longer for Paris to get dismissed with all the paperwork. Not that she remembered much about it. Ronnie and Gary took care of everything. As soon as Paris got home, Ronnie put her in a comfy gown. "I'll just be in the other room if you need me."

"No, just go and let me sleep. I'll call if I need anything."

"If you'd rather, I can check to see if Gary can stay with you."

Paris mumbled assurances that she would call Ronnie if she needed anything. *Everyone just go away. I'll be fine!* Pulling the comforter over her head, she promptly went to sleep, emitting a soft, purring snore.

Much later, when she woke up again, she realized that she felt a little hungry and a lot lonesome. Maybe she shouldn't have been so hasty to send everyone home. "Come on, Frenchie. Let's get to the kitchen. I feel like I've been gone for days. I've missed my computer and being connected with my friends! Blogging is so addictive, Frenchie, and life was so dull before I found SFF."

She flipped on the kitchen light, went to the cabinet, selected and opened a can of soup, and poured it into a glass bowl, nuking it for a couple of minutes. Rummaging through the fridge, she looked for something a little sweet to round out her meal and found some Jell-o.

Frenchie let out two small barks and a little growl.

"I've missed you most of all, Frenchie! Come on, boy. Come sit with me while I log on and update my friends. I bet they think I've died or something."

11/8/06	Yeah, I Am Still ALIVE

> **I arrived at the hospital outpatient clinic this Wed. Am about 10AM. My procedure started about 11:30. My sister brought me and my elder son took a vacation day at work to be with me. WENT RIGHT TO La La Land! OUT LIKE A LIGHT! It was not general anesthesia, but it doesn't take much to knock me out. Once I got home, I went back to sleep. I was so hungry when I woke up. I devoured my feast of chicken broth and strawberry jello. YUMMMMMM! I just wanted to write a little something to you, my friends, to let you know I am fine and did not croak! I am headed back to bed in a few minutes! Thanks again to all of you for your wonderful friendship, and prayers and good wishes~ Hugs, Paris**

"Good morning, Frenchie. Oh, please get off me! You are way too heavy. I'll let you out in just a minute. No! Quit licking. Your toenails are sharp, and I'm still not feeling well. Let me get up and take another Benadryl. I've lost track of how many I've taken lately because of the itching. The doctor said it was due to the jaundice and that it should be better with the stent in. Well, I guess I'm feeling a little better than I was."

She pushed herself up to a sitting position, slid her slippers on, and made her way down the hall to let Frenchie out. Standing at the sink, she filled the coffeepot with water. Looking out the window, she took stock of just how well she was feeling: still itching, but not as much, still tired and weak, but better. Yep, maybe today would be better. Once the coffee was ready, she took her cup and some toast and made her way to the media room, got all comfy on the couch, and flipped on the TV.

The sharp ring of the phone startled her. She must have dozed off again.

"Hello? Yes, this is Paris. Yes, I can come in on Wednesday. Why? Redo some tests? Okay, I guess. Is anything wrong? I know the doctor will talk to me, but can't you tell me what this is about? No? Okay, I'll be in on Wednesday."

After getting home from the doctor's office that Wednesday, Paris spent several hours on the net, researching. Despite reassurances from the doctors, she wanted to be informed about various cancers, what caused them, treatments, and prognosis. Others may say she was just being silly or borrowing trouble, but she knew Murphy on a first-name basis!

Dear Friends,

I went in Wednesday morning to have the test redone. Well, today they got the results. The bilirubin was down but the indicators for cancer were still high! I said, "From what I have been reading about cancer of the pancreas, it seems to run in families mostly,

and no one in my family has ever had it.
Do you think that the problem is there?"
He said no, more in the bile duct area. He
wants to consult with the surgeon, who did
my gallbladder, but he also scheduled me for
a biopsy of the liver bile duct area. That is
schedules for Tuesday Nov. 28th. May I again
ask for your prayers, and or good wishes?? I
am a bit scared, but know that I am "Saved"
and I am at a good place in my life. Whatever
is God's Will! Love, and Hugs, Paris

11/22/06   Your Response Has Touched
                              My Heart!

Wow, what a wonderful outpouring of love
and friendship you all have given to me! Just
know I have read and cherish each and every
one who so lovingly responded to my Health
Update and Prayer request. How Can I not
be ok? I will, no matter the outcome, because
I am not alone! I have God, My Boys, My Five
Grandchildren, My Sister, Lil' Frenchie and
all of you, my dear, dear Friends! Thank you
again with all my heart! - Hugs, Paris

PS, If I do croak, do ya think I could have a
cyber memorial service in the Gazebo?

Chapter 11

12/ 01/ 06 11:32 pm   **Dearest Friends**

I wish it were better news, but PLEASE know that I am not afraid, and I am ready for whatever God has planned for me. If I need to fight, I will fight. I know that your thoughts, love and prayers have been with me through this ordeal and will be. I am so thankful for your friendship. The Doctor called me about 4:00 PM. Friday. He said he had bad news for me that the results were malignant. He could not tell from the sample what stage it was. He had called and given the findings and had conferred with the surgeon who took out my gallbladder in the last part of Dec. 2005. I am supposed to call him Monday and make an appointment ASAP to see what needs to be done. He will probably recommend an oncologist. I pray I can keep my spirits up and still be silly and the sometimes naughty Parisdreamer that you all have come to know. Sorry for giving this to you so straight, but, I felt that you would probably want to know and I wanted you to get it from me and not second hand. I love you all! Hugs, Paris

Well Dear Friends, **Bad News**

I wanted to just continue to be silly and naughty and not have to tell you this, but, I don't think you would want me to bear this burden and not tell you. I just have to share with you the awful truth that I learned today. When I went to the surgeon last week, he said that he wanted me to have a PET scan to see if the cancer had spread anywhere else. He said that the operation that would be required on the bile ducts would be rough under the best circumstances. He said if it had spread there was no need to operate. I went to see him today to get the results. My dear sister was by my side, as she has been thru this entire ordeal. It has metastasized. It is in both sections of my liver, my pancreas and the top of my stomach as well as the bile duct. He said there is not much that can be done. Radiation will not help, only Chemo. He then recommended an oncologist to handle my treatment. He said it looks like I may have from 6 months to maybe 10 months. I am still hoping for a miracle. That is what it would take to save me now! I don't think that I told you but about three months ago before any of this came about, I awoke from a powerful dream. I was in a cold sweat! All I remember was that I heard a male voice say, STAGE FOUR I could not get back to sleep. Later I told my sister. Naturally she poo pooed it! Then about two months ago, she said I looked so pretty she wanted to take me to have my picture made. (My current one on the blog and my profile) Something made me say, "Well, Hon, if I should die, this is the one I want in the paper." I didn't have a real good one of me as a blonde! Then, when she sent me to Fla. at great expense, I said, "Ya know, if I should die, this is one of the best experiences of my life." When a handsome gentleman requested a special song for me and sang to me as we danced and kissed my hand, I told him that that was one of the sweetest memories that I would have. I truly think that that "DREAM" or premonition was God's way of preparing me for what was coming, because, when the poor doctor was breaking the news and said where all the cancer had spread to, I said, "So, What stage cancer is it?" He said, sadly, "Stage Four Cancer" I looked at my sister, and said, "I KNEW IT" and started laughing. Even she could not help laughing when she looked at the weird look on the perplexed doctor's face! (Sorry, guess you would have just had to be there!) I think that is why I have not cried once; I have not really been sad, or mad! There is something else that makes it a wee bit better. I was a "POSSIBLE" for Multiple Sclerosis. And one of my aunts died from complications of Parkinson's disease. When I get under stress, my head starts shaking and my hands like Katherine Hepburn's did. So, Really, I would really rather know about how long I have and go out quicker than to go in either of those two other ways. My two fine sons are, as you can imagine, having a very hard time adjusting to this and processing it. So is my dear sister. Before I started writing my blog here and developing as an individual person, I was not really that likable. She loves the person that I have become. We have only become close and have truly liked as well as loved each other this past year and a half. I owe you and your acceptance of me for that. I thank you again, my dear friends for your love, prayers and continued support. But, when we are in chat, let's play and be silly and a bit naughty, OK? I would rather not talk of it in chats. - All My Love, Paris...

Chapter 12

Paris sat down at her computer with a hot cup of sweet tea. Somehow, she found the tea a little more comforting than her normal beverage of choice. She reminisced that her mother would always fix hot sweet tea and toast when she or her sister was sick. It always seemed to cure what ailed them. "Somehow, I just don't think that it will really help me now."

She had had an exhausting day but wanted to post something uplifting for her support warriors. She reflected on how the days just seemed to fly by in a blur now. It seemed, if she wasn't taking care of Frenchie, going to the doctor's, or posting online, she was asleep. She just couldn't get enough rest to feel better. But, oh, she really didn't want life to pass her by.

"If only ... no! No if-onlys," Paris stated sternly. "I will not let this take away from who I am! Well ... who I have become. Even Ronnie seems to like me. Let's see, what shall I write that might bring a smile?"

Selecting the font, size and color, Paris began to type:

12/14/06   Dearest Friends, Oncologist
                        Gives Glimmer

I went to the Oncologist today for the first
time. I liked him! I heard that was very
important. I went in somber, but as the visit
wore on, the Dr. told me he might give me
some progesterone for something, I forgot!
Then Naughty Paris made an appearance
and said, "Oh, Doctor, will that make me
real horny???" He cracked up! My dear sister,
who accompanied me, put her head down
and her hand on her forehead and eyes full
of embarrassment, but she had a big smile! -
Hugs, and MUCH Love, Paris/Venus

12/20/06   Dear Friends, First CHEMO

I was so scared and concerned about,
CHEMO!!! Whoooooo same as boogieman!
Got a call while I was in the shower today,
raced for the phone. A woman said, "Would
you like us to reschedule your Chemo?" I
said, "Reschedule, I just called in to see when
it is going to be scheduled!" She informed
me it was scheduled for today. I said well
how about tomorrow, or the next day and
the next. She called the Hospital and they
said they were working a short Friday and
could I come right up and they would still
take me! So, I put "it" in gear and threw my
clothes on and went by myself. I knew that

I could call my dear sister to take me and
that she was wanting to take me and be with
me, however, her hubby, my brother-in-law,
was just diagnosed with Prostate cancer and
his appointment for surgical and treatment
options was today. There was no way I was
going to call her away from being by his
side today after they left there with all that
news! So, off I went. I had to walk quite a
way from the parking deck up to the main
entrance. They took one look at me when I
went to the information desk and the ladies
ask if I would like a wheelchair. I accepted.
That made the trip much easier. Everyone
was so nice. They have lunch every day.
Deli type sandwiches, fruit and chips and
dessert. They were all saying bless you, and
God's will, and all that...so, felt that I was
in the right place. They carefully explained
all the meds. I admitted to the sweet man
attendant who administered the Chemo and
to all my needs, most before I even asked,
that I was a little frightened of all the drugs!
He told me he had a nice lady for me to meet.
It was the social worker! She comforted me,
held my hand and made suggestions as to
what to tell the older grandkids. She spoke
of God, which is nice in this politically
correct world. Seems like everyone that I
met did...I felt they were my angels! (IT was
St. Vincent's Hospital) She also thought I
could get help paying the balance that
Medicare did not pay! Tom, the nurse or

Chemo attendant, don't know his title, got me ice for my coke and later made me hot tea! He waited on me hand and foot (Well, he did the same for the other patients!). OH, the 160 degree blankets he wrapped me in! LOL The other patients were nice as well as the administrator. I guess apprehension was the about 95% of my fear. I seem to tolerate my drug cocktail just fine! In fact I was so concerned because I have been so weak! I just wondered how much weaker could I get from the Chemo? Would I have to CRAWL home? Well, the later it got, the BETTER I started to feel. In fact, instead of going home and going to bed, I went to Sears to pay my bill, bought a few pretty sale items for "POOR MOI" and got my sons, daughters-in-law, and Grands all Sears gift cards. As I was checking out, the precious black sales lady looked at my hand, which was carefully bandaged to save my IV needle in my hand so they can just connect up the tubing and Not have to stick me again, and said, "Oh, have you been to the Doctor's?" I told her, No, that I had just been to my first Chemo session at the Hospital. She said she would pray for me! HOW nice is that? Then I went to the Dollar Store to pick up some supplies, gro. etc. Next I picked up an Oriental Chicken Salad from Wendy's. I went home, still having quite a bit of energy, and called my sister and recounted the above to her happy, but almost unbelieving ears!

Then I chatted with the regulars in chat. I even had a "CYBER Session" with a guy, just to see if I still, "have it!" Lol! Hope the big guy upstairs understands! Don't worry, it is someone that has been trying to get me for a while, cyber speaking. Lol! I have known of him over a year. Not a stranger! Well, here it is 1:48 my time here. Hope I still feel good tomorrow. I have to be at my Wed. Chemo session at 10:30 am! Good night, friends. Your prayers are working, big time! Can I admit something else to you?? I was picturing the drugs killing all the nasty cancer cells. I feel like they knocked of 1/6th of them today! How do I figure that, you may ask?? Well, if the Doctor is going to give me a session of three days, wait 3 weeks and three days again, and then have a scan to see if it is working. If it is, I expect it to be all healed and GONE! If not, then he said we are back to 6-10 months! Six days of Chemo treatment, so, I am believing that today we killed 1/6 of those nasty things! Can we all say, "AMEN?" - Love you friends! Hugs, Paris

Paris could hear the phone ringing and hurried to get inside the house. Between being so tired and an aching back, she barely made it in in time. She dumped her keys and purse on the counter, grabbed the phone, and sat down with a relieved plop. While saying a breathless "Hello," she reached down and pulled Frenchie up in her lap.

"Paris, this is Ronnie. Are you all right? You sound so out of breath."

"I just got back from the doctor's and was trying to get in and answer the phone."

"I'm so sorry to make you rush. Doctor's? Are you all right? I didn't know you had one today."

"Slow down. I didn't. I hurt my back late last night and wanted to check and make sure I was okay."

"How did you hurt it?"

"I was … ummm … having a cyber session."

"Well, all that sitting and writing blogs just can't be good for the back."

"You really ought to get out more, Ronnie. Now, why did you call?"

"Oh, yes. I wanted you to spend Christmas with us. I know you don't feel like decorating. I already have the decorations and two trees up, food bought, and all the stuff. You could invite your boys and their families. I would really like to play Santa to Chuck. I know you really don't feel very good, but, uh …"

"I know, it might be my last."

"I meant it might be fun. I'll come get you. Let's not think about the other."

"I would really love that. A family Christmas." Paris hung up the phone, grabbed a glass of tea, and headed to her computer.

**12 /21/06   Dearest Friends, Christmas
                              at Sis' House**

I want to wish all of you the Merriest Christmas, EVER! And the Very Best New Year! I am going to spend the Holidays with my sister and her family. My sons and families will be coming, also. Her house is

much larger and is all decorated with many decorations and lights. I am a bit weak but and looking forward to seeing all of them! My family Christmas party is Saturday morning from 11:00-2:00 for lunch. Today was my third Chemo session, then rest for 3 weeks, and then three more days, having lab, once a week during that time. I tolerated it fairly well, better than my fears had conjured up, anyway! I hope you all have a lovely time whatever you do! Thanks again for the Love, Support and Prayers! Hugs, Paris

2/29/06   Dear Friends, Update

I just wanted to touch base with you and tell you what was going on. I got back home from my Sister's house on Thursday. My Son followed in his car and carried in all the "stuff". He spent the night. So Friday, Tonight is my first night alone. ('Cept for Lil' Frenchie, of course!) I went to her house last Friday. Saturday, was our family Christmas party. It was going to be at my niece's new house down the street, but the plans changed at the last minute, and it was at my sister's house. I was able to look pretty good, CONSIDERING! Lol. Lots of comments like, "She doesn't look sick at all!" My dear lil' hubby had an old saying that seemed to suit what followed. He would say, "Hon,

You went down like a one egg puddin'!"
(Now, imagine a soufflé made with one egg.
Pfffftttt as the air goes out of it!) That is
what happened to me, my energy, and all. I
was later on the couch. When all the rest of
the folks left about 2:30, we spent our private
time together. I was able to walk around
the little pond at my Sister's house with the
kids and grandkids. (With a Son on each
arm!) Lots of things were said that needed
to be said! A Very Special PRECIOUS time! I
have to tell you that after my fairly easy time
from the Chemo, I thought I was just going
to sail right through all this just as easily!
WRONGGGGGGG!!! I experienced all the
ugly stuff. Nausea, vomiting, diarrhea, and
got to where I could not eat or hold down
anything. For a while I could eat white foods,
mild. But, Friends, It was bad. Got weaker
and weaker. I was so glad that I was not at
my house and alone. Tues. was my first lab.
My Sister took me there. I was so weak! I
honestly, would have had to get better to
die! I asked to see a nurse. It turned out, that
I was badly dehydrated and they gave me IV
fluids, 7/Up and give me strength and about
a gallon of saline solution! They also gave
me samples of medicine to put on my tongue
that melt and is for nausea. Later that night
I was able to eat crackers. The next night, I
was feeling great and cooked supper! What

a change! YEAH 'Roids! Lol Thank all of
you for keeping me in your prayers! I love
all of you and hope you all had a wonderful
Christmas and will have a Happy New
Year! - Hugs, Paris

Chapter 13

1/9/07   Dear Friends, A Brief Update
                              On My Situation

I went for the third lab and to see the
Oncologist. This ended my third week
rest between my Chemo treatments. I
don't have any lab results yet. Will check
back tomorrow. My Chemo is set up again
beginning tomorrow, My BIRTHDAY,
LOL, Happy Birthday to me!, and then
chemo again for the next two days. Then
we will go through the 3-week rest period,
having lab once per week. Then the Doctor
said I would have another scan to see if the
treatments are working. I just got approved
to get a $1200.00 per month Special fairly
new drug, Tarceva (Spelling??) free from the
drug company. The Doctor said that <u>would
make the difference.</u> (I qualify because of
low income.) Last night I started losing my

long blond hair! Today was my appointment with the Wig and support organization, New Outlook, through the hospital where I take my treatments. The hairstylist has been volunteering there 10 years! She styled the new blond wig that they had given me on my first Chemo treatment day. She feathered it around my face and made a zig zag part, and feathered in some bangs. She said, "Honey, please don't wait to cut your hair while it is all coming out!" I asked her if she would mind if I put it in a ponytail and would she mind chopping it off for me. She said that she wouldn't mind at all! Well, zip, zip, snip, snip and before I knew it, she had styled what was left of my hair into the cutest, flirtiest hairdo that you have ever seen! When my sister picked me up to go to the doctor with me, she was amazed! Thanks again for your Prayers. I am convinced that is why I have had no pain! I hope you will keep me in your Prayers and good thoughts! I will say a Prayer for you as well! Hugs, Paris

1/12/07   Dear Friends, Brave or Brazen

Tonight I finished up my third day of this second session of Chemo. I will now rest for three weeks, having lab once a week. Then comes the big "reveal" ... another Scan! This is where I expect to see my miracle confirmed! I was getting hungry thanks to my steroids and anti-nausea meds. I thought, humm, now what do I want most to eat? I decided it was ... Shrimp Gumbo from The Oyster Bar. A successful Neighborhood Bar and restaurant. I had been there many times before with my lover who was one of my bosses and 20 years older than me. I had him between my two husbands. He had driven by my house and stuck a birthday card in my door Tuesday while I was at Chemo. I had called him last week to tell him of my condition. I was afraid if I croaked he would read it in the obits that he starts his day out with and die of a heart attack! He was shocked to say the least. He is now almost 83 and, well, getting weaker all the time. A bit forgetful also. I don't want to get anything started back again with him. But while I was at the oyster bar, I started to get take out and go home. I looked around and after parking and climbing the steps to the back entrance I decided to eat in. I looked around and it was nice families and folks who had just gotten off work. I found a small table at the front and sat there and ate all by myself. I am no longer afraid, nor do I care what folks will think. (Now for my friends who have kept up with me, you may remember when last year, my niece and her husband were playing in a little club only a few blocks from my house and I would not go alone because of what I, a woman in a club alone, might look like I was looking for! LOL! I really wanted to

go, but was too afraid!) I just am not afraid
anymore! I even got brave or brazen enough
to ask the waitress to see if anyone had a
camera phone to take my picture and email
it to me. I said I would pay $5.00! She found
one guy who had a camera phone but He
did not know how to email the picture! OH
Well, I am trying to get a picture of my new
hairdo. It looks a little bit like MM! Yeppers!
Sooo cute... hope it stays in a while longer! I
love you all! - Brave, Brazen Paris! Lol

1/14/07   Dear Friends, Been Going Thru
                       a Bad Down Time

I finished my 2nd round of 3 days of Chemo
on Thursday. Friday I was able to do some
shopping, Pay some bills and run a few
errands for my upcoming trip to Deborahsu
and RusDur's wedding in Texas on the 20th!
I am leaving on the 19th. I will be returning
late Sunday night the 21st. I am better
prepared this time for the ugly aftermath of
the chemo, which hit late Friday night. I had
on hand anti-nausea medication, Gatorade,
bottled water, Chicken Broth, Chicken
noodle soup Ginger ale, Etc. (Oh Yeah, and
plenty of PEPTO BISMOL! lol) I slept until
4:30 Saturday and my son called to check
on me. His wife was gone, but suggested
he come stay with me. I was so glad he did
because despite all the preparations, and the

fact that this time is not as bad as last time, it is still PLENTY bad! Almost feels like you are dying. And I would be a bit afraid if all alone! I slept off and on today until around 7pm! I have been feeling a bit better and should be much improved by tomorrow! Love to all, Paris

1/17/07   Yes Friends, Best Laid Plans

Despite my precautions not to get dehydrated, it happened. My last Chemo was Thurs. And I was doing ok till late Friday night. Son came to help take care of me. I had the right Gatorade, got buttermilk, etc. But the nausea meds did not work right and I threw up what I ate. I could not even take my regular meds, like potassium, blood pressure, Thyroid, etc. So this morning was my regular lab. I was low on red blood so they gave me a shot, but, when I told them I really hadn't been able to eat in 4 days they sent me to my hospital as an outpatient where I get my chemo. I was to get nausea med. and steroids and saline then they got my results of potassium back and in addition to the 2 hours it took to run those fluids, they added 4 more hours for the Potassium to drip. I was there until almost 7:30 tonight. I drove myself there and back but was wheeled in and out. Now, How does Miss "I choose to be happy for the rest of my life" put a positive spin on this?? Easy! You see I am on Medicare and disability for several reasons. My income is so low that that hospital takes the balance off as charity! I could not ever afford to have treatment of any kind otherwise. If I have to go to that hospital, I get a private room. I am treated with great care, love and respect. Not like a charity case! The social worker came in to see me, and told me to have the doctor go on and prescribe the best nausea medicine for me even though only about 6 pills are a hundred dollars. She said that she would help me get them through the hospital pharmacy! She also ask me if I needed any more meds, I told her about the only prescription medicine that I take that was a true hardship was my koo koo medicine Lexapro which was about $85 dollars a month. She said it would be easier for her to send me a check for that so I could get it at my drugstore. She said she would send me a check about every other month for $100.00 to my house! Then the wig lady came into see me and recommended a shorter wig and brought one in. I thought it was really cute. (I had lamented to her that my beautiful cute, sassy hairdo was coming out in handfuls!) She promptly placed an order and is trying to get it in by Thursday for my trip to RusDur and Deborahsu's wedding.) What is good about my losing my hair, you might say?? Well, the same poison that is killing the nasty ole cancer cells is causing me to lose my hair! Yipppeeeeee! (HOW'S that for accentuating the positive and trying to eliminate the Negative?) Lol! I love you all! Paris

1/18/07   Dear Friends, Able to Eat

I have been so sick I thought I might never eat again! Lol (I always thought I would like to be Anorexic, but have come to understand it and would really not.) But thanks to all the fluids and steroids, and anti-nausea meds... Not to mention the 4 more hours of potassium I had to have today, I was finally hungry and felt that I could eat~ Now, the problem was WHAT??? I went to the lab this morning as they requested to check my potassium level after receiving the 4 hrs. worth last night. It was still low so I had 4 more hours of potassium plus anti -nausea med. in IV form. When I got out it was about 4:30. I went to Krogers. What was the first thing I saw when I entered, that took my eye?? A big shopping basket of flowers on sale! I spicd a dozen Peach colored roses! They were just beautiful. I had to have them! Lol (They were only $3.99!) I looked at the Deli section. I decided on rotisserie chicken. I was able to talk them into selling me one half a chicken! Lol I then thought I needed a salad. I bought a pkg. of organic baby field greens with herbs. I got some small sweet tomatoes to go on it and a ripe avocado. I bought a few other items to take on my trip. Dried tropical fruit, cracker sized sliced cheese and some whole-wheat crackers. I also bought stuff I knew my daughter in law liked to drink and eat. I got some soup. So my supper was rotisserie chicken and salad with lemon juice, Olive oil and garlic salt for the dressing and I added mozzarella cheese. Several hours later I opened a can of Italian wedding soup. I ate 1/2 the can and later finished off the other half! (Italian wedding soup has tiny white things in it like matzo balls and little tiny sausages, spinach in a chicken broth ... don't knock it until you have tried it! lol) Well, can you tell I am feeling better?? A bit more spunky and perky? I have to be at lab at 8 am in the morning! They will check my potassium level again. I may have to have ANOTHER Friggin' 4 hr. Drip!!! I have now lost 2 days getting ready for my trip time! Awww Nawww? Are you going to ask "Miss Happy For the Rest Of Her Life" What is good about that? Yep, I thought so! Well, I got beautiful roses now, instead of going off on a trip, being weak and maybe having a heart attack. They said my level was that dangerously low! I had a wonderful meal that I might have taken for granted any other time. I have kept it down so far... I am happy about that. Think of what that Italian wedding soup and all those field greens would…. Oh, Never mind! Love you all. Hugs, Paris

PS I want you to know that I read each and every comment you make to me. IT is what "nourishes" me with your love and friendship.

━━ Chapter 14 ━━

1/18/07   Dear Friends, Ms. Happy
                 Ain't too Happy

Note to Self - Amend happy all the time
policy! Well, just a little. You see, there
are times when life hands you a blow and
the only sane response is disappointment
or sadness! Like if you lose a loved one!
Nothing too much to be happy about!
The trick is to give the circumstance you
are dealt the proper emotions given the
circumstances. Then don't dwell on it, or let
yourself become bitter or angry over things
that you have done your very best to do,
yet failed. You must move on! So what the
heck am I talking about? WELL, To Borrow
a phrase I like from Sycamaria ... Well,
Crappy Doodle! When I went back to the lab
this morning, I was lower on my potassium
than I was before they gave me the IV's

Tues. and Wed.! So, they gave me 6 more hrs. today. I was also low on magnesium! They are going to have to check me again in the morning and if it is still low after the meds they pumped into me today, I will be in there receiving another 4-6 hrs. worth tomorrow! To add to the mix, I came down with a bad cold last night (Wed). I have been miserable all day! They did not hesitate but put me on antibiotics right away! Anything like that can be dangerous to the Chemo patient whose immune system has been knocked down! Throw into all that the weather threat and it was just too daunting a trip to try to go to Deborasu and Rusdur's wedding Saturday. I might be able to make it there, but what if I became very ill, and could not get back because of the weather? I don't want anything like that intruding on my dear friends' wedding! In that case it would be a distraction and detraction. I called off my trip. So, Yes, My Dear Friends, I am SAD tonight! But, I am breathing much easier knowing in my heart that I am doing the right thing. I will be fine and hope to see all my friends another time soon! So, "Miss Happy For the Rest Of Her Life," makes the statement; sometimes the only appropriate response is sadness and disappointment! But, Hey I will get over it! I must now try to get me well and take care of myself. I love you all! Hugs, Paris

When Paris posted the amendment to her happy statement, she took time to reread some of her posts. It was truly amazing how much her life had changed. Forget the big C for a minute. No, maybe not. Even including the big C, she could grasp how much her character had changed. Looking back, it seemed impossible to have been that self-centered, that unsure, that unhappy; allowing childhood hurts to color all of her thoughts about relationships. Yet, with just a single choice, a leap of faith, an adjustment of attitude, she had become a woman who enjoyed life—even in the midst of a battle with cancer. She had developed concern for others and confidence in herself. She now had many good friends to support her and a sister to love. And pride—the good kind. She had learned she had a talent for writing. She could share herself in such a transparent way in her blogs that others felt hopeful and encouraged. Despite all the negatives of life, all the Murphys in life, one could laugh and be just a little bit naughty. Who knew? And just look at how many views she was getting! She was one of the most popular bloggers on the site. "Okay, Lord, forgive me. That may not be the right kind of pride. But I know you understand me and love me! You led me to this point. And don't you think it's just a little bit cool?"

1/26/07   **Dear Friends, Tomorrow**
                     Will Be A First
                     1443 Views

You remember how afraid I was of the dreaded unknown CHEMO??? Ewwwwww! Well, I have that down pat. Three days of feeling great thanks to the steroids and anti-nausea drugs, and then Whammo almost a week of feeling like... Well, you know! But I must admit this week I have felt very good.

Just weak. I went to have lab again today (Thurs.). They found that my blood platelets are so low, I have to get a blood transfusion tomorrow! Now, I must admit just those words strike fear in my heart. I think of all the tainted blood, etc. All the scares! But, I have decided to do with it, like I did with the new Cancer drug, TARCEVA that I finally got up the nerve to start taking three days ago. After reading all the bad side effects from it I was frightened. To top it all off, in the lab, the other day was a lady whose face looked like she had dipped it in boiling oil! It was red, swollen and all broken out like the worst case of acne you have ever seen with third degree sunburn on top! I had read that a rash was the most common side effect of that drug. I asked on another day if that was a side effect and was told privately that it was! Most folks do not have as severe reaction. Some type rash, usually on the face happens in about 75% of the people who take the drug! There are other bad side effects, but the doctor seemed to think that this drug might make a big difference in my case. It is supposed to somehow block the growth and in a lot of cases shrink them. So, the first day that I took the pill and every day since, I say a prayer before I take the pill asking that it be blessed and accepted by my body to do its job with the least amount of side effects possible! I plan to do that tomorrow before they start that blood into my veins. I will also pray for blessings for the kind soul who donated the blood!

Hugs and Love to you all! Paris

How was your week??

1/27/07   Yes, Dear friends, Two Bags Full

I received Two pints of blood today! (FRI I only thought about one bag!) Oh well, I made it just fine ... well Except I fell sound asleep and woke up Strangled, in a coughing fit with three attendants standing worriedly over me! They were afraid I was having a stroke! It was that I had strangled on some acid Reflux! Whew that scared the chit out of them and me! Lol Other than that it went just fine. Oh, and guess what? I am being kidnapped Saturday! Yes, I am taking Lil' Frenchie out to stay with my son and his family and then going over to my Sister's house. From there, NancyL, and Belle La Donna, and Yellow Duck are getting me and taking me for a wild time in Hot Springs. Well, we will go play pool and listen to some music, maybe even dance and eat then we will spend Saturday night and they will return me to my Sister's house and I will spend Sunday night there. I am anxious to see her; she was gone for 10 days on a road trip and cruise and then turned around and went to Nashville, TN to see her daughter. We will go together to finalize the arrangements for the travel benefit trust account that AneMac has so thoughtfully started for me! Love to you all, and hope you have a swell weekend as well! - Hugs, Paris

1/30/07   Trust

After My big weekend in Hot Springs with my friends, NancyL, Belle La Donna, Yellow Duck, Fooled Once and Cinderella, and a Phone visit from Mrs. RusDur, our own Deborahsu, I am staying a few days with my Sister. Today, (Monday) we went to the Bank of America in Little Rock, AR. to set up the benefit/contribution account for my last wish, travel and or comfort fund. This is due to the enterprising, AneMac! She felt everyone would be more comfortable if my sister was the trustee for my account rather than her. But she was the instigator and ramrod for it. She did all the initial work! I really am so grateful to her! All the necessary details are in her blog, Pen Power, AneMac. I asked the lady at the bank if I would know who all contributed. She said since folks would be sending amounts from all over and from their different banks there was no way to tell me. So, if you should want me to know, you may send an email to me at Parisdreamer10 at the hotmail place and I will send you a thank you note. Just PLEASE know that anyone who sends any amount will be appreciated equally! And if you can't send anything, a sweet prayer would be appreciated! I thank all of you! I just wish I could thank each and every one of you individually for your prayers, and good wishes and many kindnesses to me! Just know that I know that the prayers are working or I would be in Pain, which I am NOT! Tomorrow is my big day at the doctor. I get a CAT scan and a report on how my treatment is going. I guess it will still be a few days till I find out what my cancer marker number in my blood is. I will keep you informed. I will write a blog telling all about my fun trip this past weekend next time~ Hugs, Paris

Chapter 15

A week later, as Paris was unlocking the kitchen door, she heard her phone ringing again. As Frenchie wiggled and jumped out of her arms, Paris slung her purse on the kitchen bar and made her way to the phone. "Hello?" she huffed.

Ronnie launched in. "I've been on the computer, and I've found a number of flights and hotel deals for five days in Paris, France. With the fund and me putting in a little extra, I think we could make it work. What do you think?"

Paris plopped down in the nearest chair. Could her dream really be coming true? Was she really going to her namesake city? She allowed herself to drift into her familiar dream.

Paris was walking down the imposing Champs-Elysees, feeling quite elegant in her cream Dior suit, stylish pumps, with complementing Louis Vuitton handbag. Looking good! She didn't think she would ever tire of the beautiful architecture and the enjoyment of the hustle and bustle of Parisian life. At that moment, a handsome older gentleman bumped into her. As he doffed his hat and gave her an old-fashioned bow, Paris noticed his thick, wavy white hair. "Je vous demande pardon," he crooned with a wicked smile on his lips.

"Paris? Paris! Are you still there? Are you all right?" Ronnie anxiously asked.

Paris yanked herself back to reality. Yep, good old reality! Bless Ronnie's heart. She couldn't possibly know or understand what it cost Paris to get up each day, let alone think of travel. As much as Paris would have loved to go to her namesake city, her practical, Murphy side knew better. If her plane didn't crash, she'd probably get there and have some medical emergency or be so sick she couldn't get out. No telling how much it would cost to ship her corpse back. Yet to be this close to her dream! Paris smiled to herself because she realized she wouldn't trade all of her dreams for the reality she now lived with family, friends, love, and acceptance.

"Ronnie, I just don't feel like it."

"But this is your big dream. All your SFF supporters have donated funds, and I can pay the balance."

"I'm just so tired all the time and can barely walk around. Truly, I'm fine without ever going."

"I could go with you, push you around in a wheelchair. Even if it was just for two or three days. If you don't go now …"

"Just the planning for it, the excitement is too much. It's really sweet of you and the SFF who set this up for me. We may need to see if we can use it to help bury me. You know that six-thousand-dollar burial plan will come due when I die, and that doesn't include a tombstone. I don't need a big, elaborate one. I'd like one, but I know I can't afford it. I just would like it to be in that black onyx like Mother and Dad's. It's very expensive, but maybe we could afford a small one."

"But, Paris, the trip! You've always talked about it. I feel so bad because I've been there and a host of other places. You didn't even get to go on that high school trip, and I did. I know I could make this work if you want to try!" Ronnie continued.

"Remember, I don't even have a passport, and it would take more time than I have to get one."

"I could get it expedited. I know I could. Just let me take care of the details."

"Leave it. I'm okay that I'll never see Paris."

"If you won't let me take you to Paris, then I'm taking you to Natchez this spring! At least we can do that trip."

"We'll see," Paris reluctantly replied.

"No. We are going, even if I have to drag your butt and cart it around!"

Paris began to chuckle. "Like *Weekend at Bernie's*?"

"I didn't mean … I mean … It's just that …" Ronnie stammered.

"It's okay. I love it. My kind of humor, you know. Oh, and by the way, on my tombstone, I want my name with my blog name, my maiden name and both married names."

"Little stone, right?" Both sisters laughed.

1/31/07   Dear Friends, Spots are Shrinking

I went to get another CAT scan today. My first one did not show up all the cancer places that the PET scan did. I went to a different place that seemed to be more thorough. They had me drink 64oz. water and then gave me an IV to hydrate me. They also used a contrast dye. I told them what the other CAT scan missed. After the CAT scan, I went home. I took a little nap, then my sister came to pick me up for a nice lunch at Julie's Place, a little restaurant with soft music and an atmosphere conducive to visiting. Then we left for my doctor's appointment. When the Doctor came in, He said I looked good. He said all my lab work; red blood cells, white, etc. were all almost up to normal from the blood transfusion that I got Friday. They joked and told me it was "Genuineeee Cheerleader blood!" Lol. They were just kidding of course but it may as well have been either that or some tough feisty ole broad's blood 'cause I sure have been feeling stronger! I feel better now than before I knew I was sick! The Doctor said that he had not studied the CAT scan much but that the cancer places looked smaller! Tomorrow I will get the results of the blood test back showing the cancer markers. Remember, it was 12,000 when first diagnosed and then after my first round of Chemo, the 3 days and then the 3 weeks rest time, the Doctor told me that it would be too soon to look for any change, but, it was down to 7,000! That was BEFORE I started the once a day Tarceva pill that is supposed to reduce growth and/or stop it. I have been taking them about a week now. My face is starting to break out a little bit! But hey, if it does what it is supposed to do! Well, it will be worth looking like a pimpled face adolescent! Lol I will let you know more tomorrow! Love to you all! - Paris

Chapter 16

I think that I have told you all before that I still have not cried, been angry, nor asked "WHY ME??" after finding out that I have advanced Pancreatic Cancer. I cried when my sister and two sons cried when I told them, but I have not cried for myself. That is very unusual, I think. But, I want to 'fess up about a pitiful attempt to persuade God, to heal me. It comes from the fact that I had been in commission sales my entire adult life. I was in Real Estate sales, Insurance, Interior Decorating (which was commission only, also) So, I caught myself, saying, "Ya Know, Dear God, all my friends at Senior Friend Finders all over the world are praying for me and are looking at my progress. I am ready to accept your will for me. If I have to go, this is a good time in my life. I am finally happy. But if I am dead and in the ground, a lot of people will feel let down and I won't get be a good witness for you like I would if You gave me a miracle healing! Besides, I have just now got this living thing and friendship thing figured out!" Then, ashamed, I realized what I was doing, and I said, "OH, My God! Here I am trying to use my pitiful sales techniques on GOD!! How Lame is that?" I said, "Please forgive my ignorance Dear God! I hope you have a good sense of Humor? Oh, Yes … You do! After all, you did make the Aardvark! Lol" - Thy Will Be Done!

Later, Paris read some of her responses.

"And bargaining with God is an absolutely normal part of the grieving process, the process of coming to terms with what life is throwing at you. Don't feel bad about it. God understands!!!! And if He didn't have a sense of humor, He'd hardly hang around with all the mess-ups we humans make in this old world as lovingly as He does!" - LizzyLoo

"Yes, I think He has a sense of humor and as He was listening to your plea He was smiling with a twinkle in His eyes." - Ola

Paris felt a moist tongue on her ankle and looked down. Frenchie made a low growl as if to say, "I'm here. Pick me up!"

Gingerly placing him in her lap, Paris began to pet him while disclosing additional responses. "Oh, Frenchie, Truehearted says God probably let out a big, hearty laugh at me getting all apologetic! I rather like that idea. He also thinks that God loves an honest prayer—and me too! He has encouraged me to continue talking to him in my own special way, because he is listening. Even to me."

Paris leaned closer to rub her head with Frenchie's, gave him a kiss, and continued. "Remember Lizzyjane from Canada? She thinks I'm wonderful and courageous and tells everyone my story. Frenchie, why are they all so wonderful to me?"

Overcome, she bowed her head. "Lord, thank you for these sweet people all over the world. I am constantly amazed at their loving support of someone most have never met. I know these friendships are a special blessing from you. I am a completely different person ... well ... most of the time, because of their acceptance and of yours. If you decide that I should come home to you rather than staying here, please let my experience help someone." Paris opened her eyes and clicked on the next page of comments and read:

> *"No doubt, many of us here will someday face a diagnosis of cancer, but you have given us the inspiration to challenge it. Should I face a similar fate, you have removed a lot of the fear, ignorance, and intimidation vis-a-vis your on-going reports." Big hug,* - Fresh Emerald

"Hmmm. God, does that mean I'm not going to get better? Could we renegotiate?" Paris chuckled. "You know I'm just kidding. But a girl has to try!"

Paris saw Frenchie patiently waiting. She picked him up gave him a little extra love and headed to bed.

— Chapter 17 —

2/2/07   My Dear Friends, Breaking News
                                    1859 Views

Stop the presses! ~ Hold the phone! ~ Wonderful news! I just heard from my oncologist office. They were closed yesterday because of the snow and ice, but called today with my latest CA19 cancer marker reading!

ARE YOU READY FOR THIS???

When first diagnosed, my initial reading was 12,000. After the first 3 days of Chemo and the three weeks rest, they did a blood test for markers. The doctor told me not to be disappointed if there was not much or any change. Well, I was thrilled to find that my readout last time was down to 7,000! Ok, are you sitting down, NOW? My reading today was......... 3,616! PRAISE THE GOOD LORD! And Thank YOU Dear Friends for all the healing prayers! My heart is full of love and JOY! - Hugs, Paris

PS, This will make the chemo Monday-Wed. and my yucky, time afterwards easier to bear!

2/2/07   Dear Friends, May Have a Date

I may have a dinner date this weekend with very handsome man. He is the one who looks like Richard Gere, only better! The one who danced with me and sang to me while looking deep into my eyes in Florida. He has a regular route all across the U.S. so as good looking as he is, it will only be dinner. I am sure he probably has a "girl in every port!" LOL He is a very nice man and a gentleman. I am looking forward to it. There is a little problem, though. My chemo should have already started, but if I had, I would be in my barfy time Saturday and the weekend, so, I asked the doctor if it would be ok to postpone it until Monday. He said "Yes, on one condition." I said, "What is that, doctor?" He said, "That you behave yourself and don't get pregnant!" lol So, I promised! Now, the big problem is this! Exactly 8 days after I started taking Tarceva, the by mouth cancer medicine, I broke out all on my face and neck. My eyes are swollen and it looks like I have a severe case of the measles. I don't look quite as bad as the lady I told you about that I saw in the doctor's office. She looked as though her face had been dipped in boiling oil. Or, like the worst case of acne with a third degree sunburn on top of it. Well, at least I don't look quite that bad yet! The doctor did tell me that they had found a correlation between the ones who got a rash and how well the drug was working. So, I must say, WELL, IT SURE IS WORKING! lol So, What should I do, warn him how I look and see if he wants to postpone or try my best to cover it up with makeup? I don't get many dates ya know, and they don't let me out much! So HELPPPPPP! Hugs, Paris/Venus

02/11/07　　Dear Friends, Rough Few Days

Sorry that I have not been online much. I sure miss chatting with you all! I also miss writing my blog. I have been kinda "puny" for the last few days. I am at home after my last chemo session by myself. It is not nearly as bad as the other two post sessions because I am not dehydrated or dangerously low on my potassium as before. This is about a 7- 8 on the yucky scale between 1 and 10, where the last ones were about a 9-10! I also have had a little complication. Lil' Frenchie was just playing around and accidentally jumped on my stomach right on top of the bad place! I have been very sore. I hope it doesn't do any serious harm. He was very sorry when I screamed out in pain! Lol Poor thing, it is a wonder he did not pee on himself! I love him, he is so sweet and loveable and such a comfort to me! I hope to be back to feeling better by the first part of the week~How was your weekend? Hugs, Paris

02/12/07   Dear Friends, Well Drats!

I went to lab today. By the time I got ready and drove there, I could hardly walk. They took one look at me and said I was dehydrated AGAIN! They did all the vitals and blood work on me and promptly sent me down to the chemo lab, which is also where you get the IV fluids. I needed anti-nausea, and saline. Lots of saline. Well, after that the nurse came in and said they had just finished up my potassium reading and it was even lower than it had EVER been. She asked me if I thought I could now hold down my potassium pills and that I needed to get down 6 of the huge horse pills before I went to bed. She said if you can't, you must go into the hospital! I assured her that I would and could, feeling that it would be possible since I had the anti-nausea drug. They asked a lot of questions to find out the cause of the problem. I did not think my potassium was a problem because I had been taking the required dosage and had caught up on my deficit. I don't want to gross anyone out but there is another condition one has after Chemo, that sort of goes hand in hand with Nausea. YA KNOW~~~~~Well it has been extreme this time. Nothing has helped. The three pills they gave me for nausea to be taken the three days after Chemo helped some but did not entirely quell the nausea. Again, I was not able to eat for about 5 days! Well, Hope you weren't eating or anything! Sorry to be gross! - Hugs and Love, Paris

Chapter 18

I love you so very much! I hope you have a perfect and Beautiful Valentine's Day! I hope you receive what you so richly deserve. Your friendship and prayers have been what has made this last year or so the Happiest time in my life. I always thought that it would take two things to MAKE ME HAPPY! #1. A Man! The perfect man, of course! #2. To be comfortably wealthy! I have neither, but, I am wealthy in Love and Friends, thanks to YOU! That is why I could not let this day go by without telling you what you have meant in my life! Happy Valentine's Day to YOU! Love and Hugs, Paris/Venus

02/15/07   Well Friends, Valentine's Day

Hope your Valentine's Day was better than mine! I went to lab at 9am and had to wait on report. Potassium was ok but they wanted to give me more fluids. Got some hemorrhoids, err, uh, I mean steroids! and nausea meds too, also looked like about a half-gallon of saline solution. The nice thing is, all the folks there got little valentine bags with goodies! There was a large box of cookies for everyone to select from. In the Chemo lab downstairs at the Oncology and Hematology lab is where I go for fluids. I go to a hospital Chemo lab to get my Chemo treatments so they can write it off as Charity. The fluid place is my Oncologist's office and practice. They have 48 Chemo chairs that are full most every time. At the hospital there are only about 10. The hospital feeds us and I get 3 pillows (3 pillows? yes, one for head, one under knees, and one under arm with IV and TIM places them there lovingly!) and 3 hot blankets! I am lucky to get one blanket at the high dollar place and no pillows are provided. You are on your own for any food or drink other than coffee or hot chocolate! Well, I hope your day went much better, but I think I have rounded the corner and am feeling much better. My friends Yellow Duck, Fooled Once, and Cinderella are taking me to lunch in Little Rock Tomorrow as, Ducky is on his way back to "Duck Pond" Mississippi! Lol - Hugs, to you all, Paris

02/19/07   Date No Show

Well, no word from my potential date who
said he would be in town the 3rd 4th and 5th
of February. He said he would take me to
dinner, have a dance and sing me another
song. He lives in Florida. I hope he is OK,
and did not get injured in the tornado! He
usually sticks to what he says. Tomorrow,
Monday, (or rather later today, lol) I go in
for my third round of Chemo. Mon, Tue and
Wed. Since my sister is back from her trip,
she has invited me to come and stay out at
her house for my Yucky time which will be
Thurs-Sunday based on past experience! I
will not be online much during those times.
Please keep me in your prayers. If the results
are similar to what I have been experiencing,
maybe this time and one more? Wouldn't
that be some miracle? - Hugs, Paris

02/21/07   Dear Friends, Getting
                                   Another Transfusion

Well my platelets are dangerously low again
so another transfusion is on for tomorrow.
At least I won't have the same fears that I
did the first time, now I am experienced!
I might want to get some TOUGH OLD
Broad's Blood. Maybe that would be good!
LOL Or how about a Marathon Runner? Just
hope they can find some good clean type A

negative blood. I have one son who has AB negative, which is very rare. Short Blog post tonight; Hope your hump day goes well! - Hugs, Paris

02/22/07   Dear Friends, Not
                            Have Transfusion

The Oncologist's office had called me Tuesday and asked me to come in early Wednesday for lab and told me it looked like I needed a transfusion. They did a CBC (complete blood count) to recheck my blood platelets. During my appt. Monday I received a shot to help my bone marrow make red blood cells. I think the name of it is Procrit? Anyway if not that, it is one like that. By Wednesday my blood platelets had come up enough that they did not have to give me a transfusion. I was almost disappointed! The one I received last time made me feel so good! Anyway my potassium is ok, but I have a urinary tract infection.

02/26/07   Dear Friends, Too Sick

Between having a urinary tract infection and Bronchitis, I am having another week off from Chemotherapy. I have mixed feelings about that. I want to get on with the business of killing those Cancer Varmints in me, but at the same time I also know that I am too weak right now to have more. It will be Wednesday before I get the CA19 tumor blood marker readings. My sister and I talked more to the doctor about the ways he could tell things were going well as far as my cancer diminishing. He said he can tell by looking at the scans and by the markers in the blood. I asked him to look again at the results of the CAT scan that he hurried thru last week. He said some of my tumors have disappeared! Some are smaller. He said progress was defiantly being made! Now you know that my attitude has been really good thru this whole ordeal, but I have almost felt like Job this last month. Usually I feel great for the three days in chemo, then really, REALLY ROTTEN for the next week. And this month was the same only I did not feel better not one day.

I had not vomited but the other problem existed almost every day for three weeks. Imodium did not touch it! Finally they gave me Lomotil and that helped. "BUT!" Well let's just say that I had to invest in Boudreaux's butt paste and Desitin ointment and still have problems. THAT is something that if it is wrong with you, no matter how sweet your nature, can really wear on your good humor. I cried out in agony to God several times over this. Not from Cancer pain, buttTTTTT you know! Lol Hope this

has not been too graphic! Bye the way, when my sister saw the shape that I am in, she is making me come to her house until the heat gets back on.

Plumbers are going to start but may not finish this week. She felt that I might get Pneumonia! So I am going to her house late this afternoon. She bought the video, Marie Antoinette for me and I will watch it on her big screen TV! Love, Paris

"Paris, I can't believe you'd just sit around and freeze to death!" Ronnie reprimanded as she stepped into the kitchen. "Why didn't you call me and let me know your heat was out before now? It has been unusually cold these last few nights, with more cold on the way. You might get pneumonia on top of everything else!"

Frenchie was yelping and jumping, scratching and being a nuisance. Paris bent over and scooped Frenchie up, crooning to him as she opened the french door to the backyard to let him run outside one more time before leaving.

"Well, I'm gonna die anyway," Paris muttered.

"You don't know that. Besides, we still have lots of sister things to make up for." Ronnie rubbed her cold arms and tried not to look around or react to the mess in the house. "I'm sorry. I really shouldn't bark at you like that. I'm just worried about you."

"I'm sorry too. I just haven't felt like doing much."

"Well, leave things to me. I picked up that Marie Antoinette movie you've been wanting to see. After that, we have to watch *Zorro the Gay Blade*."

"Remind me, why is that?"

"'Cause you've got to understand my sense of humor if

I have to get used to yours. It's only fair. I just love the one-liners! 'Know me, why sink me, once we were wombmates!'" Ronnie doubled over with laughter. When she looked to see if Paris was laughing, she said, "Okay, you'll just have to see it. We'll pop popcorn. You can eat popcorn, can't you? We'll have some Junior Mints and a good ol' time! Oh, and we have to plan our trip down to see the homes. I've already called and made reservations. It will be a great adventure. Maybe not as great as Paris. You know … if you would like to try, we could still swing that trip." Ronnie glanced over and tried to read Paris's expression.

"No, Ronnie."

"Well, the trip to Natchez will be just the thing."

"We'll see."

"It's freezing in here. Hurry up. Let's get Frenchie to Gary's and get you to my house before dark. You may stay up all night, but I'm not a night owl, and we have lots to do." Ronnie was determined to be cheerful, despite how awful Paris looked.

She loaded Paris, her stuff, and the dog into the car and tried not to notice the weight Paris had lost or the sallowing of her skin. It scared Ronnie to think how fast the time had flown since the first doctor's appointment and the prognosis of six to ten months.

Chapter 19

Another week and a half had flown by. Paris had returned to the Berkshire house once the heat was on. She reflected on the quietness here, even with Frenchie. When she stayed at her sister's house, there was always something going on: grandchildren playing, doors slamming as her brother-in-law would go in and out to work on various projects, phones ringing, pots and pans banging as meals were prepared, extra plates being placed at the table because extra guests for dinner popped in. It was chaotic.

"Come on, Frenchie. Let's go to the computer and post something to my friends. I was getting used to all the noise at Ronnie's house, but it just added to my exhaustion, and I never seemed to have time to get on the internet. Everyone will want to know about my appointment today. Okay? Okay. I missed you too while I was away. Calm down, though. I just don't have the strength to play."

03/08/07   **Dear Friends,**

Not much to tell and am a bit tired tonight.
This finished up my fourth Chemo session! I

go tomorrow and get 4 hrs. of IV fluids to try to help ward of the bad dehydration that has been happening. I am going to get enough anti-nausea med. by IV for 2 days. Which will get me thru until my lab Monday. They will also give me a lot of saline solution. This is a new tactic to try to help counteract some of the ill effects that I seem to have in spite of all my precautions! - Hugs, Paris

The next day, when Paris returned from her trip to the oncology facility to get fluids, she put Frenchie outside. Next, she poured herself a cup of strong tea and nuked it. Sipping on the steaming, sweet restorative, she let Frenchie back in. She made her way to bed, sat on the edge, and used her last bit of strength to pick up the phone and call Ronnie.

"Ronnie, I just don't know that I can make our trip. Why don't we just cancel?"

"No way! You didn't get to go on this trip in high school, and it has always been a sore spot in your life. I let you give up on going to Paris, but there is no reasonable excuse not to go to Natchez! I can get you there and back."

"I'm just too tired to get things together."

"Don't worry about anything. I'll get a wheelchair to take you around in, and you can play the grand lady with her servant. I'll even come pack your bags for you. If you are going to feel bad anyway, it may as well be in a place where you've always wanted to go. Besides, it's already paid for, and we can't get our money back. How about it? Our first sister trip! It will be great!" Ronnie cajoled.

Paris hung up the phone and pulled Frenchie close. "My sister really loves me! She wants me to have this trip to remember, whether I'm dead or alive." Paris chuckled, thinking how Murphy could have a field day with this one. She fell back on the bed without even undressing, pulled the covers over her head, turned on her side, and quickly went to sleep.

03/16/07   Dearest Friends, Valley of Death

In spite of my doctor's caution that perhaps it would be wiser if we postponed my chemo treatments yet another week, I told him that I wanted to do it and that I did not want to wait. Well, the three sessions went fine, as I have shared with you before, the days I go to chemo, I feel fine. (BECAUSE I get anti-nausea meds and steroids) It is the week afterwards that it all comes down, up, or "out"! Lol. Well, we tried to counteract the way I usually react and suffer a week then go back to lab and get fluids. They started fluids and anti-nausea meds and gave me potassium the Friday after my last Chemo treatment on Thurs. to fortify me for the weekend. My son spent Friday night with me. Even with this preventive measure, I was totally "zonked" for the next almost 4 days, sleeping virtually night and day with only about 3 or 4 hrs. a day being awake. I was a home by myself then, everyone was sick with colds again. By Tuesday morning and time for my regular lab apt. at my oncologist, I called and told them how bad I had been and still was so they sent me to get fluid and my lab work at the hospital outpatient services where I take my chemo. I was so weak that my brother-in-law had to come get me to take me to the treatment (because my sister had an appointment) and I had to be pushed in a wheelchair going and coming! My sister picked me up and took me back to my house. She had planned to take me to the Natchez Mississippi tour of the old homes and we were to leave WEDNESDAY! The plans had been made, the money paid! She threw stuff together along with my suitcase, and packed up Lil' Frenchie's stuff to take that evening to my son's house. I was weak and not too with it. But, away we went to her house and to get ready to leave the next morning. I was barely conscious. LOL. THIS HAS BEEN THE ROUGHEST SESSION YET ON MY POOR OLE BODY! My skin is almost cooked; I have a layer of dry skin like a tan peeling! My hair is almost all out now, just a few long sprigs. Do I save them like a bald guy with a comb over, or do I shave my head, like a badge of honor? (Hey, does anyone want to date a half dead, bald, scaly woman? Here I am, come get me baby!) LOL Will rest tomorrow and write about our road trip which was almost like the dark comedy, "Weekend with Bernie". Hugs, Paris

Friends, Road Trip Part #1   **3707 Views**

This would not be complete without the background. When I was a young teenager,

I was in the Y-teens. They were having a bus trip to the Natchez Pilgrimage. That is a tour of a lot of the beautiful antebellum homes. The folks are all in period costumes. I was looking forward to going with all my heart. I stayed up very late the night before ironing my clothes and packing, etc. When I woke up, it was very late in the morning. Too late to go to school and the bus had already left several hours before for the trip. I went into crying hysterics and threw a hissy fit! I was so mad, my mother said, "Well, you shouldn't have stayed up all night!" I never got over it. After I was grown, married and had children, my Mother admitted that she had slipped into my room and turned off my alarm clock so I would not get to go because she couldn't stand for me to go that far away from her. Two years after that, Ronnie, my sister, who is two years younger than me, got to go with NO problems, Mother did not care that she went. Just wished her a good time. All this time, I think Ronnie has felt a bit guilty for taking the trip that I so wanted to go on! So, back to the present time. My sister is trying to see that I get to do as many things as I really want to do, as they may be my last wishes. She set up this trip about 2 months ago and made all the plans and arrangements. She said, "I am going to see that you get to go on this trip, one way or another, if I have to push your butt all around in a wheelchair! We

are going! Whether you are conscious or
dead!" I think I said, or she did, it will be
like the dark comedy, *"Weekend with Bernie"*
where all the folks wanted to come for a
big weekend party and they find the host
has died. They know if they call the police
the party's over, so they prop him up and
pose him all weekend! Well, as it turned
out, that was almost the case. It was the
Tuesday two weeks after my chemo; I had
to be pushed in a wheelchair up to get my
IV fluids, and Potassium. My brother in law
picked me up and took me, my sister came
to get me. I had slept for almost the whole
week before that. She brought me home had
me lie on the bed and point to what to take.
She threw everything together including
Lil' Frenchie's stuff and picked up a loaner
wheelchair from my next-door neighbor,
which had belonged to her late father, and
away we went to Ronnie's house. I went
to bed and to sleep. She packed and loaded
everything. The next day we were on our
way! - Hugs, Paris

Road Trip Part #2   4915 Views

On the way to Natchez we stopped for a little
bathroom break and some refreshments in
Monticello, Arkansas. When I got out of
the car, I smelled a wonderful BBQ. Smell!
YUM! AT THIS TIME, I will NOT tell the

name of the place. It will be a whole 'nother chapter, because of our experiences on the way back. So, we went thru the drive thru and got BBQ pork sandwiches! My sister made the comment to the man at the window that if they were as good as they smelled we would come in and get "the works" on our return trip home. They were so good that I did not much mind that it caused me much internal distress and that it made several "reappearances" when we finally got to Natchez at about 4:30 that afternoon. The problem was not with the sandwiches, but with my gimped up digestive system! We had time to rest and freshen up and go to the first event. It was The 75th Anniversary of the Natchez Spring Pilgrimage from 1932-2007. When we arrived there was a crowd, cars everywhere! My sister was concerned about me. I told her to just pull right up to the door. She did. Leaving the car running, she hurriedly got out and got the wheelchair from the trunk. A very nice Southern Gentleman came to assist. He told her where to park and then wheeled me in, front row center just behind the railing. There was a seat that was saved for my sister. We were both "dolled up" for the night out. He was flirting with me! Lol. He was also in the "flag raising ceremony" at the end of the play...Ahem, No comments, but you can read my thoughts. It was the Historic Natchez Pageant. The garden clubs puts it on and all are volunteers. By even some junior high school productions it would be rather amateurish, but that also is what gives it such charm. Life before the Civil War is portrayed by what seemed to be at least half of the town's children and many grownups. It really set the mood for the whole trip and for the tour of homes that we were to see the next day. I was totally exhausted the next day and just wanted to stay in bed when the day rolled around. My sister said she would push me everywhere so we were going; she had already bought the tickets, which were for a certain color tour. 4 houses were in the tour. I was feeling so bad that after the second house I told her I could not go a minute more, I had to go back and take a nap and rest. The homes were nice and very interesting and just the type of thing I really enjoy, but at that point I was just "enduring" them. We headed back to the motel, and I got comfortable and went to bed. I said this has been fun but why don't you see if you can exchange the two tickets you have left for two homes tomorrow and instead of buying another tour of 4 homes, let's see two and go home. I have had fun for the most part but I just cannot make it! She said they would not do that. I said look on the tickets, there are probably no dates. There weren't. I said all they DON'T want to do is to give the money back. If you ask to exchange these two tickets for any two

houses on the tour for tomorrow and explain why if they have any human decency they ought to do it! So she went, and they did! Tomorrow a wonderful day, and "MYYYY HOUSE" - Hugs, Paris

"Did you have any trouble exchanging the tickets?" Paris asked as Ronnie came through the motel door.

"No, you were right. As long as I was exchanging and not asking for money, they were fine. Especially after hearing the sob story. I was much more convincing when I realized you really must be exhausted if you gave up in the middle of seeing all these gorgeous homes you've been wanting to see for all your life."

"You still don't believe it, do you?"

"I think it's more that I don't *want* to believe it. It's just so much easier to remember the manipulative you. I'd better get dressed for the wedding if I'm still going."

Ronnie showered, dried her hair, put on makeup, and was dressed and ready to go in fifteen minutes. Paris was still propped up in bed with the TV remote in her hand and eyes closed—just like she had been when Ronnie went for her shower.

"Paris, I really do feel terrible leaving you alone. Are you sure you don't mind? They really don't know that I'm coming to the wedding. I could stay with you, and we could watch a movie."

A second cousin was getting married in a little town about an hour away. The bride was the daughter of Paris and Ronnie's mother's twin's youngest son. Ronnie thought it would be fun to surprise them with relatives from home showing up. Besides, it was being held at a posh resort, complete with white peacocks. Just the type of function Paris would love to see for the architecture, décor, decorations, and bridal attire. It seemed like fate when it coincided with their trip to Natchez. Getting the most out of time and money was one of Ronnie's favorite combinations. Previously, Paris's exhaustion from treatments just hadn't seemed real to Ronnie. Sometimes she still doubted. Sometimes she wondered if Paris was up to her old tricks and using the illness to get the attention she always desired. But that was before Ronnie saw just how much it took for Paris to do anything, before Paris gave up on her dream trip to her namesake city; before giving up on seeing more beautiful mansions.

"As long as I don't have to go, I don't mind. I just want to stay curled up in bed or maybe lie still and watch something good on TV. You can tell me all about the wedding when you get back. Just try to take note of all the details I like. I'll be fine."

"You're sure you'll be okay? I've showed you how to call me, and if you need me for anything, I'll be right back."

"Mmmm," Paris mumbled as she drifted back to sleep.

Dear Friends,   **Road Trip Part #3**
                               4837 Views

On our way to Natchez, we were traveling in the rain and clouds. Our second day that was so bad was about the same...But..... The next day, the sun came out, the air was clear, and it warmed up JUST enough! It was absolutely Beautiful! The Azaleas were in bloom as well as all the other pretty posies. I woke up with more strength than I had had in several weeks! I felt absolutely glorious! (See, friends, that is the thing with this terrible disease, you can feel at death's door one day and fabulous the next???? weird!) My

sister was so glad I was feeling great! We got ready and went to the first "potluck" substitute house for the tickets she had turned in the day before. As we drove up the winding dirt hill to the property the steep banks of the road looked ancient! There were ferns growing down the banks. It was interspersed with all manner of blooming trees. Redbuds, Dogwoods, etc.! Breathtaking. The road was located on the original 90 acres and as the house came into view, tears filled my eyes, I felt like Scarlet, going home to TARA! I kept saying "OH MY GOD, OH MY GOD! I was so happy! This was everything I had dreamed of and hoped for! Everything my eye saw was pleasing to my soul! I was able to slowly walk there instead of have to use the wheelchair. When we went inside, I was astounded at the lavish decor. It had the largest collection of Sevres Porcelain that I have ever seen anywhere. There were pieces everywhere. The old china that had been original was matched by a matching company and the dining table was set with OLD PARIS China, white linen napkins with handmade lace! Above the table was an old fan that used to be pulled by servants. The drapes were sumptuous! If I died and was in heaven this would surely be a mansion that was decorated just for me! I found out that MONMOUTH as it is called is owned by a couple in California who have lovingly restored it to all of its former glory and I expect well beyond. They bought the house, which had been stripped. It was built in 1818 and was the last great mansion built in downtown Natchez before the Civil War started. It was the home of General John A Quitman, an early Mississippi governor and hero of the Mexican War. There are little out buildings that look a bit like "servants" quarters that are a part of the bed and breakfast that is there. The outside gardens were the finest I have ever seen. There are meandering old brick lined walkways lined with pea gravel and a pond with ducks and an arched bridge, that leads to a gazebo! If I never saw another mansion I would be totally happy after seeing this one! I was ecstatic! We did however make one down the road, named Linden. Thomas B. Reed who was the first elected senator from Mississippi built it circa 1800. It is still owned and occupied by a descendent of the second owners. It is operated as a bed and breakfast also. It was nice and interesting but after the first one, rather anticlimactic! We had already packed and checked out when we left the motel earlier, so we were off on the trip back home. Our mood was light and VERY happy for the lovely day. We sang old songs on the radio from the 60's and also sang, "She'll be coming round the mountain when she comes!" WE sang joyfully, and loudly and VERY badly and off key but hey.... ROAD TRIP, BABY! Yeah!

Dear friends,   Road Trip Part #4

To review or catch you up if you missed it, on the way to Natchez, MS. My sister and I had a "bathroom break and refreshment stop" in Monticello, Arkansas. When I opened the car door I smelled the best BBQ smell that I have smelled in a long time. We went thru the drive thru window and ordered two chopped pork BBQ sandwiches. My sister told the nice man at the window if it was as good as he had told us it was and that it smelled like it was, we would stop back by on the return trip and come in to eat and order "the works". I have been on a quest to find a replacement BBQ for one little place we had gone to in Little Rock, for about 20+ years. Friends, I don't know if you are as picky about your BBQ as I am, but I am. A lot of sauce is too sweet for my taste, too thin, too vinegary etc. Some of the meat is not chopped pork, but pulled and has a lot of fat on it... so far none is just right like my little Tom's 12th street BBQ. The man who owned it died and the property was sold. Well, NOW THE BIG REVEAL, as they say on the TV show where they move the bus and show the families their new homes... The name of the place was... PIGGY SUE'S BBQ! Can you hear us singing "She'll be coming round the mountain" "YES, LOTHIE, I know that is a much older song than the 50's and 60's but we were singing that before we found a station that played our music. We also were singing as we crossed over back into Arkansas, (still, loudly, badly and very off key...) PIGGY Sue, Piggy Sue, We are coming to get your BBQ!!!!!! (Of course to the tune of Buddy Holly's Peggy SUE!) We sang it over and over making up more and more verses as we went. Then we were giggling about what the décor should look like on the walls. We could see buxom cute pink pigs, in black felt Poodle skirts and black n' white saddle oxfords. We could see the boy pigs in Leather jackets, aka James Dean, all painted on the walls. Which would be adorned with old records and other Memorabilia! We were having a fine time. When we got to Piggy Sue's BBQ it was about 4pm. We were the only customers. The black man from the window was eating and there was a friendly older waitress who had been with the owner forever! When we first entered we were amazed at the lack of decor. It was clean and very nice but could have been a restaurant for any kind of food. The restrooms were spotless! They were playing the perfect music, though... all the good ole early cute rock n' roll songs. I selected Onion rings and pork BBQ salad from the menu. The man at the window had already given us a preview of the fabulous onion rings the time we went thru the drive in! OH MY GAWD! They were fantastic, only one other time have I hadn't had any rings nearly that good and it was with my "Hot Springs 6" friend at a combo, gas and convenience store near Arkadelphia. They were so good; I made a "pig out of myself" On them and took the BBQ salad to go! My sister had them also and agreed they were fabulous. The menu was very extensive. It made you want to try some of everything because it was sooooo good. Well, then my eye, caught "Fried Dill Pickles" but it was not cheap. It said like 4 for about 5 dollars. For some reason, I was envisioning slices fried dills. I just teasing and told the waitress who had been visiting with us, that I sure would like a sample. She brought us out one at no charge and it was a huge dill pickle with the same delicious batter as the onion rings, it was served with a combo mixed up of ranch dressing and their BBQ. Sauce! YUMMMMMMMMMMMMM MMMMMMMMMMYYYYYYY! We got to telling the employees what we were seeing as a cute decor for their place. We found out that they had had a fire about a year before and that is just how the contractor had decorated the place. The waitress then said she wished we could talk to the owner. In less than 5 minutes later, a black caddie drove up near the door (not in a parking space) and a large but attractive man got out and came right on in. When I saw where he parked I told my sister that I would bet anything that that was the owner~Sure enough it was.

He came to talk to us. He said he had been researching the BBQ places in Little Rock, and had come to the same conclusion that there were NO MORE good BBQ places. He has a daughter and grandkids in LR and said he has wanted to move here. The waitress told us to share our ideas with him and we did. He listened intently! He did say that he has the name Piggy Sue's BBQ registered. That was good because it was just too cute! Well, friends, this just added so much to the last day of our road trip. We got to my sister's house about 7 pm. I would not take anything for the wonderful Road Trip and even closer bonding that my Sweet, Dear Sister and I had! Thanks Sis! Love and hugs to you all, HEY want some BBQ or French Fried Onion Rings and Dill PICKLES? (Hear the music for Peggy Sue) Well, Piggy sue, Piggy sue, go on and get ya some BBQ~~~~~~~~~~~

Chapter 20

03/20/07   Be it ever so humble, there is
                  nooooOOOOHHHH
                  Place like HOME!

Well, My sister took me to the doctor's appt.
that I had today. While she was bowling this
morning, I got impatient to do something to
my thin, partially bald wispy remaining hair.
I got the scissors and started WHACKING...
Now I am talking about on my head! Lol.
One of the things that I dreaded most about
My cancer and treatments was the day I
would be Bald. Thankfully it has come
very slowly compared to most others I have
spoken with. I thought my sister would
have time to run the clippers over my head
when she got back, but was running late
so that did not happen. I went ahead and
put my makeup on and a big pair of Silver
earrings. DANG, I looked GOOOOOOD! It

looked more like a radical fashion statement than what it was! My head is (No brag, just fact!) a perfect shape. My ears are rather flat to my head and sort of cute. So, it looked good. My sister was quite surprised when she walked in and saw me and said, THAT looks really CUTE! So away we went to the doctor's office sans my wig. The Doctor's mouth dropped open when he came in the door and he pointed to my head and said, "I, uh I like that!" He saw my nice make up, earrings and big smile, and he said "You look too good to be sick!" The reason that I have felt at "death's door" this past two weeks is that I am in need of a transfusion. YEAH, let's go find the same cheerleader who gave to me last time! I felt great for two weeks! He said I would have my new cancer numbers in a few days. I will report them to you ASAP! My sister took pictures of my new "doo" on her cell phone while we were in the doctor's office before he came in. I will post one as soon as I can. Love to you all, and thanks to Yankee Girl for keeping you all updated. Thanks for your continued prayers, I KNOW THEY WORK. Now, I am praying for my TV to resurrect itself. IT went Kablooooooooooie on me the day I left home. - Hugs, Paris

03/22/07   Dear Friends

Tim, My sweet oncologist technician and Nurse, likes to tell the ladies that they are getting "Genuuuuuuine Cheerleader Blood" and the Gents that they are getting "Quarterback blood!" LOL Well, it sounds good. Oh, to have that much energy! Well today I received two more pints of blood. Felt some better today and had an excellent appetite. After Chemo, I went to Sears and went in and bought a little TV set. It took a long time because I just sort of "crept" around. Wonder if they were observing me in the security room? I was soooooo slow, and had to sit a lot, but finally did the deed. I had them load it into the car and off I went. I stopped at Catfish City and got a small catfish dinner with green tomato relish, slaw, fried taters and hushpuppies, to go. I had a wonderful supper, and a call from a very good friend of mine and we talked for a long time. I was able to "schlep" the TV inside myself and connect up the rabbit ears to it. YEAH, A TV! (Comforting background noise. I don't feel quite so lonely!) My son is working two jobs and did not bring Lil' Frenchie home, so I am really lonely. I sure am glad that I have all you wonderful friends only a mouse click away to chat with! - Hugs, Paris

03/23/07   Dear Friends, Bad
                            News Numbers

I promised you that I would post my new
CA-19 tumor marker numbers as soon as
I got them. Well, of course, I thought it
would be nearly gone biased upon the way
they had been going down. Well, the latest is
8,378! The other tumor markers, that I don't
understand, went from 5.3 up to 14.8! They
had taken me off of the Tarceva about 3
weeks ago because of the persistent diarrhea.
The Oncologist wants me to start them back
now, every other day. He is changing my
Chemo from going 3 days once a month with
a three-week rest to going every other week.
With one week rest in between. He is adding
another Chemo med, called Camptosar
along with the Gemzar. I was also getting
FU5 (which makes me smile when Tim, says
it. He is my cute technician) and some kind
of platinum. I also get a steroid, and anti-
nausea meds. (There is one other I forgot
the name of) I just got off the phone with
my sister, I called her first before posting
this to you. She reminded me this may be
some sort of test to see if I will turn from
my faith. If it is, we (I am counting on you
all and your Prayers for me) all need to fight
the devil like hell!

PS, I feel like this fight deserves some big ammo, so I just ordered a Pizza H*U*T Supreme with a salad! LOL - Love, Paris

03/25/ 07 1:53 am   Two Short posts tonight, err, uh, this AM.

#1. I am convinced that they gave me a transfusion of the wrong blood. Why do You think that? I was supposed to get more cheerleader blood. Why do you think you did not get it? I felt wonderful the last time I got a transfusion, and did for about two weeks. I had a lot of energy. Why do you think it is different this time? Because I still have no energy and have not been doing cartwheels around the room in naughty underwear! So, if you did not get the good cheerleader blood, what kind do you think you got???? GENNNNNNUINEEEEE COUCH Potato Blood!!! Probably from a redneck, white sox, blue ribbon beer belly 300 lb. Saturday morning quarterback! Reason for that assumption? 'Cause all I want to do is lay on the couch and watch TV all day! Well, Thank you Ms. Parisdreamer for your candor. Certainly! Anytime, oh do you have any tater chips with you???

#2. I am somewhat less lonely because my son brought Lil' Frenchie home this afternoon. I am so happy to see him. He did

do a second look at my baldhead. So did my
son! But hey, I could not just leave it trimmed
like I had it the other day. Oh, NOOOO, sure
it was so cute, and I felt perky, but it was not
THE BALD look. So, I kept on cutting and
then I shaved my head! I still have a perfectly
shaped head and cute ears. But, I have to
admit, it sure looks weird! Oh well, "they"
say even the worst haircuts look better in a
couple of weeks! LOL

03/28/07   Dear Friends

I went today for my new regime of Chemo.
I was feeling a bit stronger today and better
both in body and mind. My knees were still
a bit like Jell-O, but I made it fine up to
the hospital outpatient Valet parking and
walked to the elevator and to the chemo
room. My oncologist added a drug to the
mix that is used primarily for colorectal
cancer. By using it for something other than
the specified Intention, it is called being
used "off label." Its primary side effects can
be severe diarrhea! Whoooopeeee! They
also administer as pre-meds, an anti-nausea
drug and MY GOOD STEROID! Yeah! They
gave me an anti-diarrhea med in the drug
cocktail of saline solution BEFORE giving
the new drug. That along with Gem...?
However, after receiving the new drug, I
was very dizzy! I stumbled like "ole Cooter

Brown" whoever the Heck he was, LOL, so they pushed me down in a wheelchair and brought my car to me. Anyway, I go again next Tuesday for another lab, at Oncologist and get Aranesp shot for making more red blood cells. And then go to the hospital for my chemo. I will then wait a week. The third Tuesday, I will see the Doctor. Hopefully this will turn the tide and make my cancer numbers go down. Now for the Chicken Spaghetti and miracle: Tricia, who is the sister-in-law of my sister, now seems to accept me as part of the big family. I was invited over to her house for dinner after chemo tonight. She knew that I loved her chicken spaghetti. She brought over a large pan of it when our Mother died and I have been bragging on it for 13 years! After Chemo, I drove to my sister and her husband's house and we rode together all of about two blocks to Tricia and Ron's house. The meal was delicious! She had salad and garlic bread with it. For dessert, she had made a large torte with cake, whipped cream, fresh strawberries and bananas. - Hugs, Paris

03/30/07   Dear Friends

I had to go in for fluids today and anti-nausea, and anti-diarrhea drugs in IV. I was again, so weak that they had to push me up to the Chemo room. Same way back down in the afternoon. I was there from 11:00 till about 4:30! I came straight home and threw up and went to bed for a nap. I am dizzy and weak. I got chills and checked my temp about 10:00 PM I had 100.5 which may not seem much, but my Normal body temperature is one degree BELOW normal due to Hypothyroidism. (Low metabolic rate) So it was like me having 101.5. That may not be high to someone else but in years and years, I have not registered much above 99 degrees. I put in a call to the doctor and in the morning there will be a prescription called in to my pharmacy. Hope everyone has a great weekend! Love, Paris/Venus

04/01/07   Dear Friends

If you are looking for me, it may say "Profile under review." I just updated a few things. For instance I put my illness in there and my newer prognosis. I also changed my body type from "Ample" to "Normal" I have gone from wearing a fat lady 18 W jeans last April, down to an 8-10 regular size. I can wear a size 4 blazer. It is because I have a very small bone structure. I can carry 20 lbs. more than someone else my size with a bigger bone structure and still look the same size! lol. I am down to the size I was 20 years ago! One good benefit of having cancer! lol (Yeah, I know that is not very funny, Believe ME! It is me throwing up and the other thing!)Well, just thought I would share. My neighbor Mitchell is supposed to be scanning in some new pictures of me to his computer to email them to me. They were the ones my sister made on her cell phone camera in the Oncologist office the day I scissor cut my hair into kind of a flat top. The day I went without a wig and it looked more like a fashion statement! (That was before I just could not leave things alone and kept on cutting then shaved my head!) I will upload them for you as soon as I get them! How was your weekend?- Hugs, Paris/Venus

04/04/07   5169 views

I went for lab at my oncologist before chemo today. I have been extremely weak. I thought that only having Chemo, for one day a week and then another the next week would be a snap. I was Very anemic today! No wonder I have been so weak! The nurse went in and talked to the doctor. She came back and said that I needed to get another two pints of blood (TODAY, Tue.) Word by her from the doctor was, even though I had been so down did I want to miss a week of Chemo? And that he felt we needed to keep after this! It looks like I may be losing the battle after I

caught HER by surprise and asked her the same thing that I asked the doctor. I said, "So does this mean I am dying? Her face dropped and she came to sit down by me and had a very sad serious look on her face. She said, "Asking your prognosis? You need to ask the doctor next Tuesday! You do know that your numbers were not good!" She was not very reassuring as the doctor was, but the last time that I spoke to him the latest numbers were not back yet. Next Tuesday, I will see the doctor and have a list of very tough questions that I want answered with me, and this time my sister will be with me! I have been a little bit down and almost frightened by this, as I was truly looking for my miracle! I still am, but this was a reality check! - Hugs, to you! Paris

Before making her next post, Paris reviewed yesterday's. She still had a hard time believing that this many people in blogland would care what was going on in her life and enjoyed reading about it. Not that they *enjoyed* what was happening, especially not when it was getting more and more discouraging, more gross, more like there wasn't going to be a fairytale ending. Yet with all the views, all the encouragement, she could not let them down. Each day was made better when she sat down at her computer and composed a little something to share with her friends. Now she was even getting phone calls of encouragement from many around the world who were becoming special friends. It was her anchor in a sea of ups and downs. It kept her from drowning in self-pity and made her look for the bright side. It was the buoy that kept her spirits up and kept her determined to be just a little bit naughty. It kept her from being afraid and alone.

04/05/07 1:24 am   **Dear Friends**
                                        5796 Views

Yesterday, Tuesday, I went for my chemo and a blood transfusion. I received two pints of blood. I woke up feeling much stronger today! My knees were not weak! My voice was stronger. (My sister said.) I did not feel like a couch potato. So no couch potato blood. I did not feel like doing cartwheels around the room in naughty underwear, or shaking my pom poms, so no cheerleader blood. So I thought about a strong tan, tough ruggedly handsome construction worker's blood coursing thru my veins! YEPPERS! That must be it! My entire kidding aside, I want to sincerely thank all the people who care enough for other people to give their life's blood to folks they will never see. The Blood Donors, whatever they may be, homemakers, couch potatoes, rocket scientist, construction workers, teachers, etc. Where would folks be if it were not for them? It is a very noble thing to do. It can make all the difference in the world to others who need blood. My blood type is A- and every time I have needed a transfusion, enough has been there ready for me! Thank God! Thank you, whoever donated my good blood! - Love, Paris

Chapter 21

Ronnie sat in the oncologist's office seating area, flipping through outdated magazines and waiting for Paris to get another shot to help her keep the nausea away. It didn't look good. Yet, when the nurse came out and asked Ronnie to step back to an examination room, she still wasn't prepared for what awaited her. Paris was sitting with her head down and a cold cloth on her forehead. Ronnie looked questioningly from Paris to the nurse.

"Paris needs to be transported to the hospital immediately," the nurse stated.

"Why?" Ronnie inquired while assessing Paris.

"The doctor feels like more is going on and needs to do some exploratory surgery," replied the nurse.

"More than the cancer? Like what?"

"He's concerned about a bowel obstruction. I've called, and they're expecting you. They will do a few tests, and then the doctor will make the decision. They will explain more when you get to the hospital. Right now, the important thing is to get your sister there immediately."

Ronnie bundled Paris up and got her to the entrance, not

believing how slowly they had to move. "I should have borrowed a wheelchair! Or maybe an ambulance!"

"It's all right; I made it. Just let me stand here while you get the car. Don't look at me like that. I promise not to die on the way to the hospital. Just get the car."

Ronnie ran to the car and brought it up to the front of the building so Paris wouldn't have to walk any further. After helping her in and buckling the seat belts, Ronnie eased out onto Twelfth Street and headed toward St. Vincent's Hospital. Babbling like an idiot about the traffic and other drivers, Ronnie kept glancing over to comfort herself that Paris was all right.

"I told you, I'm not croaking yet. I just have blockage they want to explore."

"I know. It's just one more thing. I truly don't know how you've been so calm and accepting through all this. Who is this strong woman, and what did you do with my sister?"

Smiling, Paris just shook her head and said, "Can you go by the house and get the stuff I'll need in the hospital?"

"Sure. Don't worry."

"Oh, and someone will need to take Frenchie to Gary's. He probably doesn't have any dog food, and I'm out, so you'll need to stop and get some."

"I've got this. Would you stop stressing! I assure you I'll take care of everything."

"I know you will. Just like you did for Mother and Daddy. Who would have thought that the baby would be the responsible one? But thinking of things that need to be done keeps me from thinking of …"

Both sisters fell silent. Neither sister could believe this time had come.

04/17/07   Dearest Friends

I am so happy to be in direct communication
with you all again! I have been up here in
Little Rock's St. Vincent's Hospital Room
#1110 since Friday, April 6th. 11 DAYS! I have
only had ice chips. I had been unable to keep
down any type nourishment in my body for
nearly a month. No vitamins would stay
down. I would throw up everything I ate,
or it would "appear as like water only out
the other...well, gross...Watery diarrhea...
SORRY! But, the point is I was so low on
all my nutrients I WAS ALMOST AT THE
POINT OF DEATH" When I was admitted.
They suspected a bowel obstruction. I had
several x-rays and a CAT scan. It was. The
surgeon who took out my gallbladder in
Dec. 2006 was again called upon. He did
my surgery on April 14, a Saturday. The
hospital had spent a week or so, rebuilding
my nutrients. I had been told I might have
to have a colostomy. YUCK! But, I didn't
even have to go to ICU! I slept 18 hours and
woke up and put my makeup and wig on
and have been sassy ever since! Really, it has
been the prayers of all of you that has gotten
me through. I am now told I have cancer
in the entire small bowel and the surgeon
opened the large obstruction, ALL WILL
DEPEND upon me being able to 'pass gas
and have a poopie! So please, let's pray for

**a good poopie, then I can start to eat, and
go back to having my chemo, which should
hold the cancer at bay! I hope I have not been
too gross! Love you all, Thanks for all the
cards, flowers, and prayers! - Hugs, Paris**

"Good morning," Ronnie said as she came through the hospital room door. She stopped to squirt disinfectant on her hands from the wall dispenser and then turned to get a better look at Paris. "You really do look good this morning!"

Indeed, Paris was sitting up in bed, looking lovely in a navy caftan with tiny white flowers embroidered around the V-neckline. She had on makeup and a very swingy blonde wig. "How do you like my new wig?" she asked. "Isn't it cute? The wig lady came, took me to their beauty shop, and let me pick out the one I liked. It was a little heavy for my head, so I asked her to thin it. Isn't it perfect?" Before Ronnie could answer, Paris whisked the wig off her head and situated a red wig in its place. "How do you like me as a redhead? Sexy, huh?"

"I thought you could only get one wig," the ever-rule-conscious Ronnie inquired.

Paris patted the page-length red wig, looked up at Ronnie with "li'l debils" dancing in her eyes, and said with a shrug, "I just couldn't make up my mind. Both seemed to suit the new me. Sooooooo, I asked if I could have both. You know how hard I am to refuse!"

Instead of getting into a huff and delivering a lecture, Ronnie laughed and shook her head. It was like she was saying, if you couldn't change Paris, you may as well enjoy her! "Have you talked to the doctor this morning? Has he said when you could go home?"

"No, but I'm not in a rush. I like being waited on. I get to sleep when I want to, get visitors and phone calls. My meals are brought to me. I don't have to grocery shop, cook, or clean. What's not to like? They don't treat me like I'm on welfare without a dime to my name either. I couldn't get better care if I was rich! The only things I miss are Frenchie and my time on the computer, chatting with my friends."

"Well, I can't do anything about Frenchie, but I brought my laptop, and I could leave it here if you like."

"That would be great. I miss being online. Look, I've been making a list of all the people who have called and who sent or brought gifts. Look at this prayer shawl and these adorable hats to keep my little bald head warm!" Tears came to Paris's eyes, but she immediately blinked them away.

Ronnie looked at the list and said, "I'll add these to your map."

When it looked like Paris might stay in the hospital for a while, Ronnie found a world map with a large United States inset and put it on a cork board to be a visual reminder for Paris of all those who loved her and wished her well. She took push pins from the plastic box on the window ledge and placed them on the map, constantly amazed at the growing numbers of pins marking SFFs around the world who had called, sent gifts, or offered prayers. Ronnie made sure the map was in the center of the shelf and the gifts were pleasingly placed on either side so all could see.

Just then, there was a light tap on the door before it swung open. A petite, dark-haired woman in a navy-blue skirt and matching shirt peeked around the corner and asked, "May I visit for a few minutes?" The white-starched neck collar announced her profession as clearly as when she said, "I'm Reverend Carlton. How are you doing today?"

"As well as expected for someone about to croak," Paris responded smartly.

Ronnie watched as the reverend's eyes opened wide. She

glanced first at Paris, then to Ronnie, and then to the doorway. Before the reverend could take flight, Paris laughingly apologized for her warped sense of humor. "I'm sorry! It's just easier joking about the inevitable, and I have a really weird sense of humor anyway. Anyone who knows me knows I look at the worst-case scenario first. Do come in. I promise not to bite—or to croak just yet."

Seeking a different topic, Reverend Carlton asked about the map. Ronnie launched into how Paris had friends all over the world through SFF and how she was a famous blogger. At that moment, Ronnie realized just how proud she really was of Paris's blogs and her new friends from around the world.

Meanwhile, Paris told the reverend, "I don't know if I'm famous; more like infamous. You ought to go on SFF and read some of my blogs."

"I just may do that," the Reverend replied. "In the meantime, may I pray something specific for you before I go?"

"Yes," Paris replied. "Pray for me a poopie!"

Shock registered on the reverend's face. She quickly pulled herself together and launched into a very lovely prayer that included this specific request.

Once finished, she stated, "That was certainly a first. However, God wants us to pray for everything, and he certainly understands the intricacies of our human bodies he created. I'm sure he understands the nature of our request, as unusual as it is. I'll be stopping by again soon to see how you are doing."

As the door closed, both Paris and Ronnie broke out in laughter.

"I guess I thoroughly embarrassed you," Paris said.

"Yes. No. I think I'm getting used to your outrageous behavior. I'm even beginning to like it. I'm so proud of how you are dealing with your illness. You really don't seem sad or resentful. I'm not sure I could be as courageous."

"Should we take bets on whether the good reverend will make it back to see me?" Paris quipped. "Especially if she reads the one about trimming the bush! Did you read it?"

"Not that I know of. What was it about?"

"You remember a month or two ago when I thought I might have a date, but he was a no-show? I was all worried about him because of the bad weather."

"Sort of. But what does that have to do with your blog?"

"You will have to read it to understand. Go fire up that computer of yours and go to my blog."

Ronnie sat down and got her computer out of her bag. Once on the hospital Wi-Fi, she went to Paris's blog and read:

BUSHWHACKED!!

Let me 'splain! I have this bush in the front that had been kept neatly trimmed and well cared for. That is until a little bit over a year ago. Since there has been no man around to care for things, it had grown Wild. All out of shape! Scraggly! Who cares? But, uh oh! There may be company coming soon! Oh Dear! I decided I must take care of things around the place. Although the bush is located in a seldom seen spot and quite out of the way, I decided it was time that something had to be done! I looked at the handy blade. Then I got the idea to try a chemical agent that I had bought a few years ago when it was priced on sale, buy one get one free! Seemed a good idea! I spread the chemical on all the unwanted areas of the bush. While waiting for the allotted time to pass, the

**limbs of the bush moved. They spread the
liquid to other areas, much more coverage
than was intended! Time came to spray the
bush off to stop the chemical action! By that
time the poor bush was almost a "burning
bush" because of the old liquid that I had
used on it. Well, the results were horrible...
Poor bush was almost totally gone! Well,
maybe the visitor won't even notice!**

Ronnie could hear Paris cackling as she read and reread the
blog. "Surely you didn't mean—"

"Uh-huh!"

"I don't think I would have guessed if you hadn't been
laughing."

"Not everyone is as naïve as you, and I mean that in the
kindest way."

"Oh, Paris, that's, uh … naughty … and well written!"
Ronnie choked out as she broke into laughter. "Did anyone else
get it?"

"I did have to give a hint to a few. Are you shocked with
your sister?"

"No. But you'd better hope the reverend doesn't read this
one, even though I doubt she'd get it."

"I wouldn't be surprised either way," Paris mumbled as she
drifted off to sleep.

Later that evening Paris posted:

05/01/07   Dearest Friends

**I have really been missing you! Sometimes
my sister will bring her laptop computer
up here at the hospital, you remember, the**

same one I use at her house... I have dubbed it as the "dinosaur?" model! Lol. I have now been here 25 days! Most folks keep asking when they can go home...not me! I know when I have a real good thing! What I use to like so much about vacations was laying up in bed, watching cable TV and having my room cleaned, etc. SOOOOO, this is like a luxury vacation to me. I have a very pleasant private room with a bath. Nice view out the big window...and the best of care, far beyond ordinary! I am comfortable and well cared for. At different times, each son has spent the night with me on the fairly comfortable twin size chair bed. My sister has stayed also quite a bit. Last Thursday, JustBelle came up from Louisiana to stay with me. She stayed until my procedure, Monday. Thanks So much, JustBelle, Love ya! Bye the way, the procedure went very well, no, complications! My liver is draining nicely. I have never smelled anything as gross in my life! I will never eat any other animal's liver again! Yuck! I also wish to thank all of you who have sent cards, letters, computer printouts of the blogs, all the sweet gifts, flowers, fancy hats, etc. You know who you are. I hope to send you private thank you notes, but hope this will be ok for now. Also, for the calls that I have been receiving from all over the world, quite literally! Thank you so much, my friends! Do you know that I could never say that I was happy? But, what is really weird is that I can truly say that now. I am happy! Yes, Even with all that is going on with my cancer and the fact that I might be going to die! I am happy in my heart, at perfect peace with others, myself and GOD! I love you my dear ones and you and your sweet thoughts and prayers have brought me to this wonderful place to be! Thank YOU SO MUCH! - Hugs, and much love, Paris/Venus

━ Chapter 22 ━

Days later, Ronnie was giving Paris a back and foot rub with Paris's favorite Nivea cream. No matter what the day brought, Paris would cover her face, neck, and arms with Nivea. A woman should look her best at all times, even sick and in the hospital. A certain doctor, X-ray technician, or gurney attendant might just be worth the effort. After all, she wasn't dead yet!

Unable to control old habits all the time, Paris muttered to herself, "It would be my luck that Mr. Right would appear just when I'm ready to kick the bucket!"

"What did you say?"

"Never mind. Ronnie, hand me my notepad. I've made a few notes about things I want done. I don't have much, but I'd like a few personal items to go to my sons and grandchildren. Also some instructions on what I want to be buried in and so forth."

"Paris, don't," Ronnie protested.

"I know you don't like to think about it, but I like to think I'm being practical. I haven't given up. You know I like to think of the worst, and then I'm prepared. It's just like when I first got here and had my lawyer friend come to make you my POA. I have to think of these things. It makes it easier for me."

"Okay, I understand. So, what else?"

"Reverend Carlton has agreed to speak at my funeral."

"Really?"

"Ummm, yeah. She's been coming in to see me each day. Can you believe it? She even read some of my blogs! Strange as it seems, I think she really gets me." A shy smile emerged. Shaking her head, Paris continued, "I've talked to my SFF friends, and they are going to give me a cyberfuneral! I told them I'd like for everyone to let a white balloon go all over the world at the same time. Don't you know that will really mess with someone! Imagine those satellites reporting strange unidentified objects floating up all over the world all at the same time? And maybe you could play 'Up, Up, and Away' on a sound system." Paris took a breath, looked at Ronnie, and started laughing. "And I need you to tell Randy, you remember my friend who embalms?"

"The tall one that looks a little like Ichabod Crane?"

"Yep, that's the one."

"What am I supposed to tell him?"

"That I want my boobs taped so they don't look flat." Glancing at the look on Ronnie's face, Paris asked, "What? Haven't you ever noticed how women look so flat lying down? Does that embarrass you? Do I need to call him myself?"

Ronnie just sat there, not knowing whether to be appalled, laugh, or cry. She just shook her head. "Just never crossed my mind, but yes, I'll do it. What else?" Ronnie asked with resignation.

"I'd like to be buried in my beautiful blue peignoir set. I've never worn it, and though it may be a strange selection, that's what I want!" Paris searched Ronnie's face for any condemnation.

"Okay, anything else?"

"I talked to AnnieMac, and she has agreed to let me use my Paris fund to help with my funeral expenses. It won't go far, but maybe it would help with my tombstone that I wanted.

I still find it hard to believe the generosity of my SFF friends in contributing toward my dream trip to Paris, like that Make a Wish foundation. They have been so good to me!"

"I'm sorry you didn't think you could make your dream trip, but the fund will certainly help. Anything more?"

"Oh, I just wish …"

"What?"

Tears came to Paris's eyes. "I just wish I'd managed better and that I had something, even a little something to leave my boys."

"No problem. I'll take care of that. It may not be much, but they'll have a little from you. And quit worrying about funeral expenses. You just concentrate on getting better."

"Thanks, Ronnie."

"No thanks necessary. That's what sisters do! Now tell me more about the Nashville Bash. Maybe you will feel more like going in a few days."

"Ronnie, I'm not giving up, but I'm beginning to think I've already had my miracles."

"What miracles?"

"For one, you know I can't handle pain. Pancreatic cancer is supposed to be extremely painful, and I haven't had any. Also, I've had the miracle of making so many good friends around the world. You and I know what a selfish mess I was before SFF. I was so unhappy, and I wanted others to be unhappy too. I have had the miracle of being happy—and of traveling. I may not have made it to Paris like I'd dreamed, but you made sure I got to Dallas, Natchez, and St. Petersburg. Without another miracle, I just don't think I'll have strength to go to Nashville."

"I could push you around, like in Natchez."

"Leave it. I don't want to dampen the good time of the others. Besides, the Arkansas Six will come by on their way there and back, so I'll get all the best gossip. Think of all the SFFs who have called or come by. Remember, JustBelle came and stayed with me a few days to give you some rest. I truly am blessed!"

"There just has to be some way!" Ronnie said thoughtfully as she paced around the room. "I know! We could make a video and send it with the six. That way you'd 'be there.'"

"Hmmm. That might not be a bad idea. I'm sure the hotel would have some way of showing it. I wouldn't want it to be morbid or anything. Maybe I could do a poll and let them pick whether they like me better as a redhead or a blonde. Let's do it!"

05/03/07   **Dearest Friends**

For those of you who may have read Justbell's blog about her stay with me in the hospital, you have a truer picture of my condition than my optimism and pride has shown before. Every day is an emotional roller coaster. One day I seem at death's door. The next day is just glorious. It has taken a toll on me emotionally. I continue to pray for the miracle of complete healing and believe in it so much that it's difficult for me to face the reality that it may not be God's plan for me. I have been in the hospital for 28 days. Because of the progress of the new stint in my liver, I have been cleared for Chemo on Friday and perhaps a permanent stent that will drain on the inside and not require a drain bag on the outside of my body. The doctor said that by next Friday (May 11th), we will know more of the direction of my future. Meantime, with all the drain bags I've had and all the holes

in my body, I thought it might be amusing
to go out in my rose garden, drink a pitcher
of water, pull the plugs, and slowly twirl
around and be my own sprinkler. Lol

Chapter 23

"I thought I was a goner," Paris recounted to her youngest son, Barry.

He and two of his children had come to see her. Paris was playing the grand hostess, entertaining with her near-death story. While her son sat on her bed holding her hand, her eleven-year-old grandson was checking out the world map. His little nine-year-old sister was trying on Paris's knit hats. Ronnie was snapping pictures and trying to give mother and son some space.

After everyone left, Paris asked Ronnie to explain the near-death experience once again.

"Tell me what happened. I don't remember a lot except I really believed I was dying."

"You have no idea!" Ronnie exclaimed.

"Tell me everything again from the beginning."

"I was so frightened that I've forgotten some of the details, but basically you got some kind of shot yesterday, and within minutes, your eyes rolled back in your head. You gave a couple of jerks with teeth chattering and then lay back, death still and unresponsive. I pushed the panic button three or four times and then ran to the nurses' station. While a team of doctors and nurses worked on you, a public-relations representative took me outside the room and told me you were dying.

"Paris, I was so angry! I kept insisting that you were having some sort of reaction to that shot, and they had better do something! Your reaction just didn't fit the pattern of death I've seen, and I knew something else was wrong. The woman tried her best to calm me. She kept explaining in a calm, even tone like you'd use to calm a child, 'Your sister has pancreatic cancer and, well, she's dying.' Like I was an idiot! 'Your sister signed a do-not-resuscitate order, and you need to accept that this is *it*,'" mimicked Ronnie.

"Oh, Paris, I was so frightened, but I was angry too! I know she was just doing her job. I'm ashamed to say, I was not very nice to her. I screamed, 'Like I don't know this? But not now! And *not* this way! Not this suddenly! Something else is very wrong. My sister is having some kind of reaction!'

"I kept begging her to listen to me and do something! I kept asking, and asking, what was in that shot?"

Ronnie continued, "She left. I don't know if she told anyone. I don't know if they finally gave you something or if you just came out of it. That's the part I can't remember. I was just too scared! I just knew I wasn't ready to lose you. Not right now, and not that way."

"Well, here I am! But, Ronnie—you know I'm ..."

"Yeah, hon, I know. Maybe we'd better get started making that video and not put off stuff that matters to you. When your next visitor comes, I'll run home and get the camera. Should we start a script?"

"No," Paris replied with that up-to-something grin, "I'll just be me!"

Later, Paris managed to type a brief post:

5631 VIEWS

Now, friends, this brings me to the sad part. With all my heart, everyday, I've been looking forward to the Nashville Bash. With each day that passes there are obstacles thrown in my way that makes me realize that it would not be safe for me to go. My health can turn on a dime as it did the other night when I experienced a rigor, complete with teeth chattering, panic, and feeling like I was having a heart attack. Honestly, I am so weak, that when I get up to sit on the potty chair, I need my oxygen and get the shakes from sitting just a few minutes. So... I cannot even conceive of the effort it would take to get dressed for even one event or the toll that it would take on my strength. On a lighter note, my sister has come up with an alternative. She thinks it would be nice if I could videotape a greeting to you all from my hospital room that could be shown at the bash. I want all of you to party twice as much, once for you and once for me. I'll be with you in spirit and I appreciate everyone's effort on my behalf for the white elephant sale, date auction, and the t-shirt sales. Drink a toast to your pal, Paris...I'd like a frozen margarita with extra salt or a good merlot wine...but you have whatever you like...lol. Love to you all, Hugs Paris/Venus

Switching on the video camera, Ronnie walked down the oncology hall, saying, "We are here at St. Vincent's Hospital. News has it that the world-infamous queen mum of the bad girls, Parisdreamer, famous and well-loved blogger, has been residing here for the past thirty days. Let's knock and see if we can go in. Paris? I see we've caught you primping."

"Yes, I'm primping for a private party," she purred. Drawing up her hospital gown to expose some leg, she continued in that sultry low drawl, "Want to see my puss?"

Slapping her legs before things got out of hand, she apologized with a come-hither smile. "The debil made Paris be naughty!" Continuing, she asked the camera, "Want to see my bald head? As you can see, I'm on oxygen." She gestured from the tube in her nose to the machine. "Here are my three tubes coming out of the side of my neck like Frankenstein. And over here I have a tube coming out of my stomach."

Pausing for dramatic effect, she indicated another tube. "And this one out of my liver. Yuck! Now let me show you my comfortable room where I've resided for this past month!"

After a short break for Paris to regain some strength and to change from her drab hospital gown to her navy-blue caftan and blonde wig, she continued, "Enough of that. Let's have some fun! I invite you to participate in a poll to decide which Paris look you like best for the Nashville Bash!"

Making appropriate facial expressions, Paris purred, "This is my shy, demure, sexy, blonde look. I raise my glass and ask that you have the best party ever! Have an extra margarita or merlot or whatever, and don't forget an extra margarita for me. In just a few minutes, I'll be back as a redhead and let you decide."

Changing her blue caftan for a goldish-yellow one, donning her red wig, and sticking a golden flower in her hair, Paris lay back and closed her eyes. After a few minutes, she opened her eyes and told Ronnie, "Let's finish while I can."

With camera rolling and in her sexiest husky, full-of-promise voice, Paris continued, "How do you like my naughty redhead look? After all, I am the queen mum of the bad girls, and I was voted as having the naughtiest blog. Of course, I was the only nominee, but still I liked it!"

Lifting her glass again, Paris proclaimed, "Here's to you. Have the very best party. You now know why I can't be with you, but I'll be there in spirit! Remember to vote on which look you like best, and always remember, I love all of you so much! Party hardy! And don't forget my margarita!"

When the camera was off for the final time, both sisters started laughing.

"I can't believe you said and did that! I was so embarrassed!" Ronnie proclaimed between bouts of laughter.

"I can't believe you didn't switch off the camera! Don't worry about it. Those at the bash, they'd be disappointed if I weren't just a bit naughty! You don't think it was too, too much, do you?"

"Like you said, they would be disappointed otherwise. You are who you are. And, after all, you are the author of the infamous 'Bushwhacked' blog," Ronnie concluded, still wiping tears of laughter from her eyes. "Was that the nomination for the naughtiest blog?"

Noticing how tired Paris looked, Ronnie suggested a nap while she ran home to finish the project. "I won't be long."

Yet, Ronnie was reluctant. She had been staying 24/7 with Paris for a while now, so it seemed strange to be leaving. She glanced at Paris and could see she was already asleep, so she quietly left.

Thinking it would be a nice touch to add a little message with the video, Ronnie sought out her son-in-law Allan's expertise to make it happen. Paris had indicated how she loved one of her cards because it was musical and played the song "I Will Survive." So, Ronnie wanted to include it with a little message from Paris, much like one of her blogs. She could just see it rolling up in the *Star Wars* style as a dramatic conclusion of thanks to her friends, with the music playing in the background:

Dear Friends *(Did you think I'd lay down and die?)*
Thank you, *(Oh no, not I)*
Again for *(I will survive)*
Your love *(Oh, as long as I know how)*
Support, gifts, *(to love)*
Calls *(I know I'll be alive)*
And prayers. *(I've got my life to live)*
Have a wonderful *(And all my love to give)*
Time in Nashville for me *(I will survive)*
Love, Paris *(Hey, hey, I will survive)*

It proved to be a powerful ending. Ronnie rushed back to the hospital with the film in tow. She hoped Paris would like the ending and that it would make it to Nashville.

When Paris woke up, Ronnie was back and told her about the delayed ending to the video.

"I just hope the Nashville Bash crew will continue to watch after the video for the ending rolling up like credits. It's about a three-second wait."

"I can make sure. Put the computer up here, and I'll post something."

05/07/07   **Dear Friends**
                                                6305 VIEWS

On a lighter note, Saturday my sister and I filmed a little DVD so I could feel a part of the Nashville festivities. It turned out to be a little naughty, a bit bizarre...yet cute and

touching. The final message is a bit delayed, so please take time to watch it. Hope you will enjoy. - Hugs and Love to All, Paris

05/08/07   Dear Friends

About 1:15 p.m. I was taken down for my liver drain to be replaced with a permanent stint on the inside thus riding me an outside drain. However, there were complications. The stent had totally stopped draining and the area had become infected. The area was cleaned of infection and the drain was replaced. It was decided to wait for another week to try the procedure to put the drain on the inside. Whatever they did has allowed me to feel somewhat better and has relieved some of the area pain. During this procedure, unfortunately, I was not knocked out completely and kept giving technical advice to all the staff which I'm sure they appreciated (Not...lol). Thanks for your continued prayer support. I came through with flying colors...feeling again like the Timex watch...take a lickin'...keep on tickin'. Hugs and Love, Paris

05/13/07   Dear Friends

Just giving my first operation scar TLC. Have not been permitted to touch the area before now. And NO...I'm not talking about anything REAL pleasurable if you know what I mean. My dearest sister is spending the night with me and is typing this for me as I dictate it to her. It helps not to have the weight of the computer on my tummy. I want to thank, Nancy, BelleLaDonna, DeborahSu, Rusdur, Cinderella, and Fooled Once for dropping by my hospital room to see me on their way to Nashville and safely delivering my wicked, naughty video. I understand the Nashville Bash was a great success and although I wish I could have been there,

I'm sure after watching the video, you can understand why I could not be there physically, but was there in spirit....Could you feeeeel me?? I pray for everyone's safety and wellbeing as they make their way home. Monday the 14th, and here I'm up for the same procedure that I've been for the past three Mondays. I had shorter notice this time, but know I must contact my prayer warriors. I love all of you and thank you from the bottom of my heart for your support, prayers, and love. - Love and Hugs, Paris

"Ronnie, are you still awake? I'm not quite ready to go to sleep just yet, and that's a first in a long time!"

"I'm still awake. You want to talk about the procedure? The doctor indicated it would be a relatively easy procedure to place the permanent stent inside, once they have the infection under control. After all you have been through, it should be a piece of cake."

"No, I'm not worried about that. I just wanted you to know what I found out. I don't want you to be upset with me or anyone."

"Paris, what in the world are you talking about? Have the doctors told you something that I don't know?"

"No, it's nothing like that."

"Then just tell me!"

"I'm on YouTube!" Paris began to laugh. "Truly, I didn't have anything to do with it. Our video is on YouTube."

"What! The video we made? Why? How?" Ronnie sputtered.

"Those who didn't get to go to the Nashville Bash heard about the video, and they wanted to see it. Evidently, it was a hit. A lot of bloggers have never seen me and wanted to see the video. The easiest way was to post it on YouTube. I hope you aren't too upset."

Ronnie closed her mouth, thought for a minute, and then began to laugh. "At this point, whatever! It will be an interesting legacy you are leaving behind. You know they say that once something is on the internet, you can never get rid of it. Are you okay with that?"

"Yeah, I am," Paris mumbled as she drifted to sleep with a smile on her lips.

Chapter 24

Ronnie slipped out of the room while Paris was taking one of her frequent naps. She passed the nurses' station, stopped to exchange trivial pleasantries, and then continued to the refreshment station. Since she'd been on the oncology floor for so long, it seemed like she was now accepted as a volunteer or part-time staff member. She was allowed to monitor and replenish the coffee machine, hunt down any supplies she or Paris might need, and was even consulted about Paris's care.

"Oh, there you are!" the patient's rep, Anna, said.

"Mmm, just waiting on a fresh cup. Paris and I both need it!" Ronnie replied.

Anna flipped through some paperwork, glanced at her watch, and then shared the bombshell, "You do know we'll be discharging your sister today, don't you?"

For a moment, all Ronnie could do was stare. Anger and fear surged, and Ronnie blurted out, "What? You can't! She's scheduled for chemo treatment here on Friday." Calming down a bit and realizing there must be some miscommunication going on, Ronnie continued, "The doctors haven't said anything to either of us, and she is still much too ill."

"I'm pretty sure of my information."

Completely dismayed, Ronnie pleaded, "She can't go to her house, and I'm not prepared!"

"I'll check on it and get back to you," Anna smoothly stated as she walked off.

Ronnie rushed to the nurses' station to see if any of the nurses knew anything about Paris being discharged. One nurse mentioned seeing Paris's doctor not long ago and that she'd get him a message to stop by their room.

Before long, the doctor came by Paris's room and, after the customary pleasantries, asked to speak to Ronnie in the hall. Trying to hold panic at bay, Ronnie gave Paris a smile, rolled her eyes, and followed him out the door. "Ronnie, you know your sister has pancreatic cancer. The prognosis was never very good. The chemo treatment has been canceled in light of new information," Dr. Smith stated.

"What information?"

"Well, you know we had to abort the stent procedure this past Monday," he continued.

Ronnie nodded.

"We found cancer everywhere. So thick we couldn't possibly cut through it. Take your sister home, make her comfortable, and let her say her good-byes."

With a quick, awkward pat to Ronnie's shoulder, Dr. Smith turned and made his escape before Ronnie could process all the implications of their conversation.

The next couple of hours were a whirlwind. A home healthcare representative came in to explain what the healthcare nurses could and could not provide. She gave Ronnie a quick tutorial on how to clean and maintain all of Paris's drains as well as the feeding tube. Watching the healthcare nurse's mouth moving, Ronnie knew she needed to listen and store the information, but her brain refused to work. She couldn't even remember the woman's name. Twenty minutes later, the woman gave Ronnie a card as she was ready to breeze out.

Coming out of the information overload, Ronnie shouted, "Wait! I'm expected to do all of that? Even the liver drain? A CNA couldn't do that! We've had to call a registered nurse every time. Now I'm expected to do that?" A sense of overwhelming helplessness was settling in.

"Don't worry. We'll send out a nurse for a few days to show you until you are comfortable doing it," the healthcare nurse cheerily replied as she moved closer to the door.

"What about hospice? Don't they help?" Ronnie said, grasping for any aid.

With a tight smile and a flicker of sympathy in her eyes she replied, "As long as Paris has the feeding tube, hospice cannot help."

Ronnie reached out, put a hand on her sleeve, and pleaded, "But it's not like she's getting nutrients. She's just not ready to give it up."

"I'm sorry. That's the policy," the home health rep murmured as she exited the room.

Slowly turning toward the hospital bed, Ronnie realized that Paris had heard everything. Paris gave Ronnie one of her most beautiful smiles and said, "I know the little girl in you wants to curl up and cry or maybe pitch a fit, but the confident teacher/woman I know can handle this."

Whoa! Ronnie thought. *She's the one with terminal cancer. The one who has just been told to go home and die? The same one I've accused of being totally selfish, and now she is giving me words of encouragement? What a transformation!* She said to Paris, "You're right. We'll get through this if the Lord's willin' and the creek don't rise."

Both sisters smiled at the reference to their father's favorite saying.

A nurse came bustling in with the discharge papers, flipping back and forth, requesting Ronnie to sign at the Xs, while reciting the discharge spiel.

Reality pushed to the front of Ronnie's brain. "But I don't have her room ready, and isn't there a way to get a hospital bed?"

"It will take a couple of hours to set up her transportation and have her ready to discharge. I'll call about the bed and have one delivered to your house along with other supplies. Why don't you go home now and ready the room?"

Ronnie arrived at home in a rush and was relieved to see that her husband, Coach, was there. She opened the back door, threw her purse and car keys on the kitchen counter, turned, and flung herself at him to be enveloped in his big, strong, safe arms. She let go of her tears and babbled her fears that she had held at bay all morning. When her emotions were spent, she roused her strength and explained that Paris would be transported to the house soon and what needed to be done.

"Oh, my gosh! I didn't even ask if you minded. It will mean such a change in our lives. I don't even know for how long, and …"

"Hush! You know I will do whatever it takes for your family. That is what love does. We saw your mom and dad through; we can see Paris through. Dry your tears, and let's go move some furniture."

Before nightfall, Ronnie had Paris situated in her new bedroom. Until now, it had served as Coach's retreat/library/office. The carved desk and a matching set of wingback reclining chairs had been removed to make way for the hospital bed. Even some of the sports pictures and winning plaques had been removed to make the room less masculine. The hospital equipment delivery people had placed the head of the bed against the ornate floor-to-ceiling mahogany bookshelves, lovingly made by Coach for Ronnie. This gave Paris a great view of the pond, thanks to the triple set of full-length windows. A black iron futon was placed on the adjacent wall to provide seating for visitors or a place to sleep for any overnighters. Paris had instructed Ronnie to stop by the family's Berkshire house and dig particular bed linens from a specific plastic bag in the corner of the master bedroom. With the blue-and-pink floral bedspread, matching sheets, and coordinating decorative pillows tossed on the futon, the room looked rather homey, considering.

— Chapter 25 —

A few days later, Ronnie heard the tinkling of the bell Paris used to summon her.

"What's up? Need something?" Ronnie asked.

Despite Ronnie's misgivings, things had settled down to a routine. The home-care nurses had been understanding and helpful. At least once a day, a nurse would show up to take care of the critical health issues of cleaning the drain tubes and changing out the feeding bags. Ronnie had been emptying and charting the outputs of each bag, taking Paris's blood and recording the findings of the glucose test. Much like at the hospital; nothing she couldn't handle.

"My feeding tube bag alarm is going off," Paris replied, "and you know if the port gets dried, we'll lose it. I don't have any more ports left."

"This shouldn't be happening. The nurse isn't due until this late this afternoon."

The beeping was not only annoying; it was causing Ronnie's panic to spike. Coach had gone golfing, and Ronnie was alone in the house with Paris.

"I'll call the nurse on duty and see if they can send someone else sooner."

Ronnie ran to the fridge and grabbed the magnet holding all the important numbers, dialed, and quickly explained the situation.

"Please hold," a sweet but remote voice said. In a moment or two, that same sweet, still-remote voice said, "I've looked at the schedule, and there is no one who can get to you in time."

"Well, something has to be done, or she will lose the port."

"You are right, but we just don't have anyone available. The bag must be changed, and the tube has to be cleaned out with heparin. The real problem is an air bubble. Yes, I don't see any other way. You'll just have to do it."

Ronnie switched to her teacher voice to get results. "I can't! I'm not trained to do that! This is totally unacceptable. You have to send someone!"

"I've told you, no one is available, honey. Don't worry, I'm going to transfer you to our nurse on duty, and she will walk you through it. Please hold while I put you through."

By this time, Ronnie realized no one was coming. She ran back to Paris's bed, where she dropped to her knees and kept repeating, "I can't do this! I can't do this!"

Paris smiled and said, "Sure you can. I trust you. Besides, it's not like I'm not dying anyway."

"Really? Really? That's what you say to me? *That* doesn't help!"

Paris reached out and squeezed Ronnie's hand, nodded, and smiled encouragement.

By that time, a soft, motherly voice came on the line, "Now, hon, let me walk you through this. Just give me a moment; I'm working in my garden and need to get to a better place for reception. There are only two things to be concerned about:

getting an air bubble in the syringe and too much heparin. Now the first thing you want to do is …"

All the time the instructions were being given, Ronnie, with tears running down her face, called out, "God! Oh, God! Please, God! Help me!"

Both Paris and the voice on the phone kept encouraging Ronnie through each step. Almost finished, Ronnie prepared to administer the heparin, when Paris said, "You know what heparin is, don't you?"

"Shush! I can't hear, and my hands won't stop shaking."

Finally, her task finished, Ronnie thanked the nurse profusely, hung up the phone, and fell to her knees, sobbing, "God! God!"

Gulping in some much-needed air, Ronnie glanced up at Paris to make sure she was really all right. Paris had her famous "li'l debils" dancing in her eyes and was biting her lips to keep laughter from erupting. Remembering the question, Ronnie gave in. "No, I don't know what heparin is. What is it?"

"It's arsenic! At least a form of it. That is why she was concerned about giving too much of it. It's poison," Paris choked out in laughter.

"Oh, my God! You mean I gave poison to my sister?" Ronnie screeched hysterically.

"Don't worry. Remember? I'm dying anyway!" Paris concluded. "But wouldn't it have made a great headline— 'Woman gives arsenic to dying sister' or maybe 'Woman shoots already dying sister with poison.'" She laughed even more at the horrified look on Ronnie's face.

Collapsing on the floor again, crying or laughing, neither sister knew exactly which, Ronnie squeaked out, "Oh, Paris, you are too much! Here I am about to … oh, forget it! I'm just glad I didn't kill you. It's good to know you still have your warped sense of humor. I think I could really like this person you've become."

━━ Chapter 26 ━━

A couple of days later, the sun was bright, the weather was mild, and the breeze was gently blowing—a perfect May day. Paris opened her eyes and saw little gnats flying around. Ronnie was diligently checking tubes and tidying up.

"Have I died and I just don't know it?"

Startled, Ronnie stopped what she was doing and asked, "What would make you say something like that?"

"The gnats."

Ronnie smiled. "No, it's just that time of the year, and the grandkids must have left the door open too long when they were here checking on you. Want to go out on the porch and swing awhile?"

"Isn't it too much trouble hauling all my bags and oxygen?

"We'll manage if you want to go."

Four bags, machinery, and varying lengths of tubing had to be loaded or carried beside Paris's walker every time she got up. Paris and Ronnie slowly made it out of the house, across the porch, and to the wooden swing, much like the one they had grown up with on Dennison Street. The sisters settled down in companionable silence. Ronnie glanced over at Paris, who had her eyes closed and a small smile on her lips.

"The sun feels so good. All the way to my bones," Paris declared. "Thanks for bringing me out here." The swing moved gently back and forth with a comforting squeak-squeak.

"Ronnie, I hate to tell you this, but I can feel them coming for me. I've been fighting it, but I'm so tired and weak."

Not discrediting Paris's knowing something so strange, Ronnie answered, "Oh, Paris, it's going to be all right. You know where you are going. You'll love seeing Mother. Let's get you back to bed for a little nap. I think Ian is coming in sometime tonight."

Ian was Paris's "adopted" son, who had been living in California for the past twelve years. He and Gary had been best friends in school. Gary brought him home when Ian had nowhere else to go. After Paris's nurturing heart found out that Ian had lost his mother at an early age and was being shuffled around with no one really taking care of him, she declared him part of her family, called him her son, and told him she would be his second mother. Even after he moved to California, Ian was faithful to send cards and to call each week to check on his second mother. In fact, when he heard that she was unable to go to visit Paris, he sent a beautiful book that had colorful pictures of all the special tourist spots, with descriptive and interesting details of each place. He had inscribed it with his love and stuffed pictures of his friends in the same envelope. He wanted his mother to know he was not alone and she was not to worry about him but take care of herself. At the time he sent the package, he hadn't fully realized that his last visit would be so soon.

Later that night, Paris opened her eyes. "Son, it's good to see you!"

As Ian leaned over to hug her, he whispered, "I don't want to lose you."

With an understanding of how it must be losing another mother, Paris smiled and murmured, "We'll both watch. How do you like my music?" A Bob Marley tape played in the background. "It makes me feel so happy, like I'm on a beach somewhere."

"I've got the same one," Ian replied. He squeezed her hand and choked out, "I love you."

"You need to tell our story someday."

"I will," he whispered. But Paris was already asleep again.

Stepping outside the room, he closed the door and gave in to the despair he could no longer deny. He covered his mouth to muffle the sounds and then wiped the tears quickly as he noticed his auntie Ronnie approaching. She took him to the kitchen nook, gave him a quick hug and a glass of ice-cold sweet tea.

"Has Gary been by?" Ian asked.

"Yes, he and April have been sharing in some of the care of Paris these last few days. They should be back anytime now."

"What about Barry?"

"He came to the hospital with his two oldest, but I haven't seen him since. He does call now and then. I suspect it is just too hard for him, seeing her waste away. You know how she spoiled him."

"Yeah, Momma has always tried to protect her children, even now. That's why I know she will understand that I have to leave tomorrow."

"Sorry you have to leave, but we all understand. I know she is so happy that she got to see you one more time. You know how she loves you."

"Yeah, I know. I'd better get on to bed. I'll be leaving early in the morning."

"Well, good night. Have a safe trip and keep in touch. I'll let you know."

The next morning, Ronnie tapped on Paris's door and called out, "Telephone. Abelle is on the line and wants to talk to you."

Paris made a sound but didn't open her eyes.

"Don't try to talk if you don't feel like it. I'll just hold the phone up to your ear so you can hear all the latest on the SFF. I think she is going to read you some of the latest blogs."

Paris's eyes fluttered and breathed soft little noises and grunts as Abelle told about the latest tidbits on SFF. Ronnie heard Abelle conclude with, "All the SFF family sends their love and prayers." Paris let out what sounded like a contented sigh.

About the time Ronnie had replaced the phone, the doorbell rang. In trooped most of the Arkansas Six. They gathered around Paris's bed and began recalling the good times. Sensing new activity, Paris tried to focus on who was talking.

How wonderful! I'm surrounded by my best friends! They came, even with sick ole me with no makeup, not able to say much or be my charming self, they came! Love welled up from inside Paris, acknowledging how blessed she'd been to know this group and admitting how much they meant to her. *Please don't forget the naughty me!* Paris thought as she drifted off again.

Later in the afternoon, Ronnie answered the door again, and this time two nurses from hospice entered. After a brief conversation and an assessment of Paris by the nurses, Ronnie signed the papers to agree to the hospice terms.

"She really hasn't been conscious for a couple of days. The feeding tube is no longer being used, so she meets your requirements."

"We will send a nurse out tomorrow to help. If you need anything before then, here is my card. Just call this number."

Everything was quiet. Paris didn't know how long she had slept. Was it hours or days? She remembered Ian coming in early in the morning to say he had to get back to California, and she remembered the Arkansas Six coming and being silly with her, recalling good times and embarrassing moments of the group. Paris opened her eyes. The room was empty except for Ronnie, who was checking her bags and tubes. Gary, who had been diligently praying, preaching, and reading from the Bible all afternoon, had just stepped out to use the bathroom. Ronnie's grandkids were laughing and playing a game in the twilight on the porch, just outside the windows of Paris's room. Ronnie moved to the door to shush them but turned back when she heard a slight sound.

Paris's eyes blinked open again, and she said, "Mother's right. There are several guardian angels who come for you."

"That's nice, dear." Ronnie moved over to the bed, leaned down, and kissed Paris on the forehead. As silent tears rolled down, she continued, "You know I forgive you and hope you forgive me."

Paris closed her eyes again and drifted.

How lovely. I feel like I'm floating like a balloon. Maybe I've died and joined with the balloons at my funeral. Wouldn't that be something. She laughed to herself. She saw Gary sitting on the futon, head in his hands, silently weeping and shaking his head and murmuring, "Why was I not in here?"

She saw Ronnie open the door and fall into Tricia's arms.

"How did you know?" Ronnie asked.

"I just did. You know how we just sense things. Ronnie, why is there a tow truck coming down your drive with their lights flashing?"

"I don't know. Hospice said they would send someone out when I called them, but I thought it would be an ambulance."

Both women looked at the truck with its hook swinging

back and forth, looked at each other, and then exclaimed at the same time, "She'd love it!"

I would have liked a limo or caddie better, but okay, a tow truck is on par with Mother sliding out of the hearse in her casket. Paris laughed.

Feeling better than she had in all her life, she realized she had to say good-bye for now. *Remember me! Oops, I'd better say our bye-bye prayer.* Paris closed her eyes and continued,

> *Heavenly Father,*
> > *Go with us each our separate ways,*
> > *Guide us, lead us, protect us, and bring us back*
> > *safely together.*
> > *In Jesus's name, amen.*
> > *I love you so much.*

Hearing sweet, melodic voices that sounded as beautiful as church bells chiming on a Sunday morning, Paris opened her eyes again. Billowing white clouds parted, and she saw an imposing structure with flying buttresses. *Notre Dame?* Next, she floated by what appeared to be the Eiffel Tower.

How can this be?

Conversations drifted up to her—all in French! Next, Paris saw quaint little shops and sidewalk cafes facing what she somehow knew was the Champs-Elysees. Paris took a closer look.

My own heavenly namesake city!

It was even more alive and beautiful than she'd ever imagined.

A gloriously handsome man of undeterminable age was sitting at the most gorgeously prepared table Paris had ever seen. It was laden with every kind of scrumptious food imaginable. The man had long, wavy white hair and was dressed in a shimmering white suit. Next thing she knew, she was standing in front of him. He looked directly at her with warm, piercing brown eyes, smiled, and said, "Come and sit at my table."

Unafraid and feeling a calm, peaceful joy flow over her, she asked, "Who are you?"

"I have many names, but to you, I am Monsieur Droit—Mr. Right. Welcome, Paris."

And the angels smiled.